EVOLUTIONARY PSYCHOLOGY

THE BASICS

Evolutionary Psychology: The Basics is a jargon-free and accessible introduction to evolutionary psychology, which examines behaviour, thoughts, and emotions in relation to evolutionary theory.

Reader and Workman outline how evolutionary thinking can enhance the core areas of psychology: social, developmental, biological, cognitive, and individual differences/abnormal psychology. Covering topics such as genetics and natural selection, mate choice, culture, morality, mental health, and childhood, among others, the book integrates psychology into the biological sciences and explains the different approaches in the field by evaluating current and past evolutionary research and theory. Key studies and theories are explored in an accessible way, with the work of key evolutionary and behavioural scientists from Darwin to Dawkins examined and explained.

Including a glossary and further reading, this is the essential introduction to evolutionary psychology for students of psychology and related areas, and academics and researchers, as well as anyone interested in learning more about this fascinating field.

Will Reader is Senior Lecturer in Psychology at Sheffield Hallam University in the UK. Previously he taught at the Robert Gordon University in Aberdeen, at Cardiff University, at the University of Glamorgan (now the University of South Wales), and The University of York, where he completed his DPhil in 1994.

Lance Workman is Visiting Professor of Psychology at the University of South Wales in the UK. Previously head of the Psychology Department at Bath Spa University, he received an undergraduate degree in psychology and biology (BA Joint Hons) from Keele University and his doctorate (DPhil) in animal behaviour from the University of Sussex. In 1990 he set up the first undergraduate module in Evolutionary Psychology at a British University.

The Basics

The Basics is a highly successful series of accessible guidebooks which provide an overview of the fundamental principles of a subject area in a jargon-free and undaunting format.

Intended for students approaching a subject for the first time, the books both introduce the essentials of a subject and provide an ideal springboard for further study. With over 50 titles spanning subjects from artificial intelligence (AI) to women's studies, *The Basics* are an ideal starting point for students seeking to understand a subject area.

Each text comes with recommendations for further study and gradually introduces the complexities and nuances within a subject.

SUSTAINABILITY (SECOND EDITION)
PETER JACQUES

TRANSLATION
JULIANE HOUSE

TRANSNATIONAL LITERATURE
PAUL JAY

TOWN PLANNING
TONY HALL

WOMEN'S STUDIES (SECOND EDITION)
BONNIE G. SMITH

WORLD PREHISTORY
BRIAN M. FAGAN AND NADIA DURRANI

DEATH AND RELIGION
CANDI K. CANN

HINDUISM
NEELIMA SHUKLA-BHATT

RELIGION IN AMERICA 2e
MICHAEL PASQUIER

EVOLUTIONARY PSYCHOLOGY
WILL READER AND LANCE WORKMAN

For more information about this series, please visit: www.routledge.com/The-Basics/book-series/B

EVOLUTIONARY PSYCHOLOGY

THE BASICS

Will Reader and Lance Workman

Routledge
Taylor & Francis Group
LONDON AND NEW YORK

Designed cover image:© H_ctor Aviles / EyeEm via Getty Images

First published 2024
by Routledge
4 Park Square, Milton Park, Abingdon, Oxon OX14 4RN

and by Routledge
605 Third Avenue, New York, NY 10158

Routledge is an imprint of the Taylor & Francis Group, an informa business

British Library Cataloguing-in-Publication Data
A catalogue record for this book is available from the British Library

ISBN: 978-0-367-22343-4 (hbk)
ISBN: 978-0-367-22344-1 (pbk)
ISBN: 978-0-429-27442-8 (ebk)

DOI: 10.4324/9780429274428

Typeset in Bembo
by Taylor & Francis Books

We'd like to dedicate this book to the memory of our friend and colleague Kevin Crowley

CONTENTS

FIGURES

TABLES

BOXES

ACKNOWLEDGEMENTS

We would like to acknowledge the support and guidance we have received during the production of this book from Eleanor Taylor, Sandie Taylor, Shreya Bajpai, Tori Sharpe, and Alex Howard.

1

INTRODUCTION TO NATURAL SELECTION AND GENETICS

WHAT IS EVOLUTIONARY PSYCHOLOGY?

If we define psychology as the study of behaviour, thought and emotions, then evolutionary psychology can be defined as the study of behaviour, thought and emotions *in the light of evolutionary theory*. Evolutionary psychologists are of the view that current behaviour and internal states reflect the influence of psychological dispositions that aided survival and reproduction in the ancient ancestral past. This means that, in order to understand evolutionary psychology, we first need to develop a basic understanding of evolutionary principles. Fortunately, evolutionary concepts are both interesting and, once explained, make surprisingly intuitive sense. To support this, we also need to develop a broad understanding of basic genetics – once again an inherently fascinating and intuitive field of science (well we believe it is and hope you will also!). In this chapter we introduce and explain the principle of adaptive evolutionary change – **natural selection** and basic genetics – before providing some history on the development of evolutionary psychology. In future chapters we consider how evolutionary psychology can be used to help us understand the main sub-divisions of academic psychology, including social, developmental and cognitive psychology. We also consider how an evolutionary approach can help us to understand romantic predilections, why people differ and why some individuals are prone to mental health problems. Finally, we look at the relationship between evolution and the development of culture. But first, there's that little matter of evolutionary principles.

DOI: 10.4324/9780429274428-1

NOTHING IN BIOLOGY MAKE SENSE EXCEPT IN THE LIGHT OF EVOLUTION

The famous Russian biologist Theodosius Dobzhansky once declared 'Nothing in biology makes sense except in the light of evolution'. To Dobzhansky (1973), trying to understand biological entities, without consideration of evolutionary processes, is only scratching at the surface. Bearing in mind that humans are biological entities, it seems remarkable that, until quite recently, the vast majority of psychologists considered that they could make complete sense of the human condition without reference to evolution. We firmly believe that in the twenty-first century the time is right to suggest nothing in psychology makes complete sense except in the light of evolution. This may sound a bold statement to make. Can we substantiate it? After all, traditional psychological approaches have been deployed to explain, for example, why boys and girls differ (social conditioning), why some people suffer from schizophrenia (abnormal levels of circulating neurotransmitters) and why some people find it difficult to maintain long-term romantic relationships (poorly developed attachment style during infancy). All of these explanations have been developed by psychologists to help us understand the causes of our internal states and behaviour; in other words, these *why* questions are really forms of *how* these behaviours came about questions (note that the first explanation stems from social psychology, the second from biological psychology and the third from developmental psychology). They do not, however, explain *why* humans have such propensities within their developmental repertoires. Evolutionary psychologists ask *why* questions about internal states and behaviours by considering the conditions under which our ancestors evolved into *Homo sapiens* (during the **Pleistocene** era between 2.5 million years and 11,700 years ago) and the adaptations they developed to help them survive and reproduce during this era. We will consider evolutionary explanations for the three questions above in later chapters. For now, in a nutshell, boys and girls gravitate to differing gender roles today due to differing reproductive pressures their ancestors faced; some people suffer from schizophrenia because they inherit certain genes which make them susceptible to this illness, given we are now put under pressures that are novel compared to our ancestors and, under the varying, life on the edge, circumstances that our ancestors faced, in order to pass their genes on, it no doubt paid them to develop a range of personal relationships.

PROXIMATE AND ULTIMATE TYPES OF EXPLANATION

The 'how' type answers that we discussed briefly earlier can be thought of as here-and-now proximate explanations for behaviour. In contrast, the latter 'why' ones we have just outlined are known by evolutionary psychologists as ultimate explanations. It is important to realise that neither form of explanation is more correct than the other. Nor is one more important than the other. To illustrate the difference, we might pose a question about behaviour and then answer it in both proximate and ultimate ways (Mayr 1961; Conleyn 2020). Many years ago, one of the authors of this book found evidence that male European Robins developed local dialects. This finding of bird dialects requires explanation. There are various proximate ways to explain this. A young bird hears the songs of other mature robins in a particular geographical region in which he grows up; he then develops a song with similar notes and phrases. (Note we might also have considered neurological changes in response to the local dialect he hears.) This sort of information helps us to understand his song development. Note, however, this answer does not really explain what is the function of having a local dialect? An ultimate explanation might suggest, for example, that having this particular dialect signals to females that he grew up in this particular area and hence is likely to have locally adapted genes to help solve the specific challenges of that environment. This makes her more likely to mate with him and hence having a local dialect has a **selective advantage**. One way of thinking about these two forms of explanation is to consider the time scale. While proximate explanations focus on what happens during the life of the individual, ultimate explanations focus on what occurred to populations over many generations. This book deals with the ultimate, evolutionary level of explanation for human internal states and behaviour. This way of looking at life can be traced back to the theories derived by a Victorian naturalist that you will no doubt have heard of – Charles Darwin. In order to understand the subject matter of this book, we need to understand what it was that Darwin did and how his ideas have been further developed in recent years.

WHAT DID DARWIN DO?

Many people assume that Darwin came up with the notion of evolution. Interestingly, however, the concept that species can change over time had been around for at least two thousand years by the time Darwin arrived on the scene. Ancient Greeks, Romans and Chinese scholars all suggested evolution might have occurred. Darwin's contribution to the concept of evolution was twofold. First, he suggested a theory for a working mechanism to explain how evolution occurred and second, he marshalled evidence to support this theory. He called this theory of evolution 'natural selection'. Although a brief summary of the principle of natural selection, as described by Darwin and his contemporary naturalist Alfred Russell Wallace, was read out to the Linnean Society in 1858, it was in 1859 that he published his famous book *On the Origin of Species*. Since '*Origin*' outlined the theory of natural selection in some detail and provided evidence that it had occurred, scientists generally date Darwin's theory of evolution back to 1859 (Workman 2014). A key feature of natural selection is that members of a species appear to 'fit' their specific environments extremely well. That is, each organism appears to be designed to cope with the challenges of its environment. Such challenges include gathering food, avoiding being gathered as food, keeping warm/cool, finding appropriate places to live and attracting a mate. In modern terminology organisms are said to be well **adapted** to the challenges of their particular **ecological niche.** Examples of this include Darwin's observation during his famous voyage on *the Beagle* of the how well giant tortoises are physically adapted to the specific challenges of different islands of the Galapagos archipelago. On more misty, elevated islands the tortoises were larger with domed shells and short necks. In contrast, on the flatter, drier islands tortoises were smaller, had longer necks and 'saddleback' shells (rolled back at the top like a Spanish saddle – see Figure 1.1). It was clear to him that the larger bodies of the tortoises on the elevated islands helped keep them warmer whereas the saddleback shell and smaller bodies on the hotter islands helped them to

Figure 1.1 'Lonesome George' was the last of his species of Pinta Island Giant Tortoise who died at the age of 102 in 2012. Ironically, his species died out because they were unable to compete with goats introduced to the Galapagos which were naturally more successful at gathering vegetation

remain cool and the longer necks enabled them to reach the somewhat higher vegetation. Although during the voyage of the *Beagle* Darwin had noted the fit between the environment and the adaptations to it, he did not at this point understand how one led to the other. It was only later back in England that he realised there is natural random variation between offspring in a population and that some of these offspring will happen to have inherited features that allow them to cope with these challenges more successfully than others. This, in turn, led to an increased chance of survival to reproduction when compared with others in the population. This in essence is natural selection.

To recap, in a population there is random heritable variation and, due to selective pressures, there is differential reproductive success. Those individuals with the best adaptations to that particular environment will survive to out-reproduce those less well suited and leave more descendents with similar characteristics. Note that there is competition for survival and reproduction with each generation and, as the environment changes, different adaptations are selected, leading, over many generations, to the process of evolutionary change.

In addition to his observations of the wildlife on the Galapagos Islands in *Origin* Darwin outlined many other examples of animal adaptations to various environmental pressures both biotic (living entities such as competitors for resources) and abiotic (non-living entities such as climate). These were based on his observations when travelling the world on board *the Beagle* and on his numerous correspondences with other experts from around the globe (Darwin wrote letters almost every day of his life following his return from his circumnavigation). He also studied animal husbandry and how breeders had greatly altered the shape and behaviour of their animals through successive bouts of artificial selective breeding (the term natural selection was derived from a contrast with artificial selection). In *Origin* he describes in some detail the adaptations to their environment of a whole menagerie of animals from anteaters to zebras. But, curiously, he only mentioned humans in one short paragraph towards the end of the book where he stated:

> [I]n the distant future I see open fields for more important researches. Psychology will be based on a new foundation, that of the necessary acquirement of each mental power and capacity by gradation. Light will be thrown on the origin of man and his history.
>
> (Darwin 1859, p. 458)

This short paragraph has proven to be both prescient and prophetic. Hence it is worth pausing to unpack what exactly Darwin is suggesting here. To begin with, by stating 'Light will be thrown on the origin of man and his history' he is suggesting, as well as for other species, humans are also the product of evolution. Moreover, by writing, 'Psychology will be based on a new foundation, that of the necessary acquirement of each mental power and capacity by gradation', Darwin is suggesting the brain/mind is a product of evolution just as much as anatomical features such as the human liver or heart. Hence, we should consider human nature with all of its qualities and foibles as arising out of selection pressures of the ancient past. Interestingly, this is exactly the view of modern evolutionary psychology as developed over the last 30 years. Note, however, he states this will happen 'in the distant future'. Once again this was prophetic as evolutionary psychology only emerged more than a century after Darwin's death (Workman and Taylor 2023).

BOX 1.1 CAN WE SEE EVOLUTION TAKING PLACE?

One counterargument to evolution is the notion that we can't actually see it happening – so why should we believe it has taken place? To be sure, most evolutionary changes are slow, gradual and difficult to trace given how brief (on a geological timescale) the human **life span** is. While major evolutionary changes can take millennia, it is however possible to see clear evidence of more minor evolutionary change over relatively short time periods. One classic example of this is the adaptive change in the colouration of the European peppered moth (*Biston betularia*) following a change in their environment. Traditionally the peppered moth's speckled wing markings help it to blend in with the lichens on the bark of trees on which it settles. As we can see in Figure 1.2, this allows for a high degree of camouflage and is therefore a good antipredator adaptation. This level of camouflage is, of course, dependent on the existence of the lichen that covers the bark of many trees in areas where the moth is found. Unfortunately for the peppered moth, due to the industrialisation of Western Europe during the nineteenth and twentieth centuries, air pollution killed off much of the lichen on trees in and around cities. This, in turn, revealed the brown bark underneath. This meant that the peppered moth was no longer camouflaged when settling on the bark of trees. Once the peppered moth became conspicuous to predatory birds it might have been driven to extinction.

Fortunately, a new mutated dark variant arose which was able to blend in with the bark and once again members of this species became camouflaged. This new variant, being more effective at survival, passed on more copies of its genes to the next generation and its numbers grew as the peppered form declined. Hence, given that observers noted all three of the factors necessary for Darwinian evolution, random heritable variation, selective pressures and differential reproductive success, this is a demonstration of evolution

Figure 1.2 Light and dark forms of the peppered moth (*Biston betularia*)

by natural selection documented over a period of decades rather than millennia.

DARWIN'S OTHER GREAT WORKS: SEX AND EMOTIONS

Having dropped the bombshell that was his theory of evolution on nineteenth-century readers, Darwin's next two books on the subject were in some ways even more shocking. In 1871 he published a book on sex. *The Descent of Man and Selection in Relation to Sex* fleshed out the concept of **sexual selection** as a second driving force for evolutionary change. Put simply, whereas the natural world does the 'selecting' in natural selection, in the case of sexual selection the opposite sex does the selecting. Darwin came up with the concept of this second form of selection because he was unhappy that the males of many species are more gaudy than their female counterparts. So, while peahens are pretty dull, peacocks are fabulously exotic; likewise for many species such as the birds of paradise and mandrills. Since natural selection drives the sexes in the same direction because both have to, for example, avoid predators and gather food, why should males be sexier than females (and literally make a song and dance about this sexiness!)? Darwin suggested that sexual selection worked in two ways. First, there was female choice where females choose attractive males because this 'sexiness' was an indication of quality. Second, males compete with each other for access to females, which might involve intimidation or outright aggression. This means that many males, as well as being more colourful than their counterparts, have also evolved greater physical strength and 'weapons' such as horns and large canine teeth. You may at this point be thinking, how does this concept of sexual selection help to explain human sex/gender differences? This is a question we will explore in Chapter 2. Suffice to say here that evolutionary psychologists suggest it forms the cornerstone of explanations for sex differences both in physical form and (more controversially) in behaviour.

The third and final book that Darwin published on evolution appeared in 1872 and was called was *The Expression of the Emotions in Man and Animals*. This book was his most psychological and explored the notion that emotional expressions are adaptations that arose through natural (and sexual) selection. This might not sound particularly shocking, but becomes more so when we realise that, in order to make these arguments, Darwin also proposed continuity between ourselves and other species in emotional expressions and that this, in turn, suggests there may be continuity between ourselves and animals in terms of our internal states. In the church-influenced Western societies of the nineteenth century this was literally sacrilege. We will return to the implications of this work for evolutionary psychology in Chapter 5.

As we can see, both of these latter books were important in the advancement of evolutionary thinking and, in particular, the development of evolutionary psychology. We will return to the development of evolutionary psychology later. First, we must consider how one major gap in Darwin's theory was finally plugged during the early twentieth century.

THE PHYSICAL BASIS OF EVOLUTIONARY CHANGE: MENDELIAN GENETICS

While Darwin had provided a theory of evolution that was well supported by observations from plants and animals (and from the fossil evidence), there was still a piece of the puzzle that was missing. This was the physical basis of heritability; in other words, his theory lacked a physical mechanism of inheritance. Darwin knew that something physical must be being passed on from parents to offspring, but he didn't know what this was. We know now that genes are passed on – but during his lifetime only one person knew about genes and he did not appreciate the importance of his own findings. This was the Austrian Monk Gregor Mendel whose experiments with pea plants had demonstrated the existence of genes in 1866. (Note that Mendel never used the term 'gene' but rather wrote about 'factors'. The term gene was introduced in 1903 by Danish botanist Wilhelm Johannsen). Although he published his findings in a small local journal this was not widely read, and its implications were not realised until the early years of the twentieth century (Darwin died in 1882).

WHAT DID MENDEL DO?

During his time at the Augustinian Abbey of St Thomas in Brno, Mendel studied inheritance in some 29,000 pea plants. Through a large series of self-fertilising and cross-pollinating breeding experiments, Mendel made three ground-breaking discoveries. These later became known as **Mendel's laws of inheritance**. First, characteristics (**traits**) such as pea colour (yellow or green) are coded by genes which act in pairs (in sexually reproducing species one comes from each parental sex cell or **gamete**). These genes can be dominant (only one gene required for the characteristic to appear) or recessive (two genes needed to show the characteristic). Second, there is a relationship between the physical traits (or **phenotype**) and an organism's genetic code (or **genotype**), but this relationship is not straightforward; it is possible for two plants to have different genotypes but still have the same phenotype. Two pea plants might both have yellow peas, but one might have two copies of the yellow gene and the other might have only one copy. This is because the yellow gene is dominant over the green gene. Somewhat confusingly, the dominant gene is traditionally allocated a capital letter and the recessive one the same lower-case letter – e.g. 'Y' for yellow and 'y' for green peas. When two copies of a dominant or two copies of a recessive gene occur in the organism it is said to be **homozygous** (homo means alike – hence

YY and yy) for the trait. In contrast, if it has a dominant and a recessive gene it is said to be **heterozygous** (hetero means different hence – Yy). Third and finally, Mendel noted that genes are 'particulate', that is, rather than blending together (as Darwin thought) they are passed on intact. This means that, for example, peas are either yellow or green not a yellowish green intermediate.

BOX 1.2 THE PUNNETT SQUARE

Following the rediscovery of Mendel's work and the rise of genetics in the early years of the twentieth century, Cambridge evolutionist Reginald Punnett developed a simple way of illustrating the various genotypes that emerge from breeding experiments. This became known as the **Punnett Square**. For pea colour, yellow peas (Y) are dominant to green peas (y). So, if we cross a heterozygous yellow pea plant (Yy) with another heterozygous yellow pea plant (Yy) this can be illustrated by the simple Punnett Square demonstrating the resultant genotype ratios:

	Y	y
Y	YY	Yy
Y	Yy	yy

Note that both YY and Yy genotypes have a yellow phenotype leading to a 3:1 ratio of yellow to green peas.

You might, at this point be wondering what do pea plants experiments have to do with evolutionary psychology? The answer is they have very little to do with psychology, but when it comes to evolution, Mendel's discoveries with pea plants instigated the science of genetics without which the concept of evolutionary psychology would have very little meaning (Plomin 2018). As we will see later on in this book, our understanding of the relationship between genes and behaviour has moved on enormously during the twenty-first century and is one of the reasons for our bold claim at the beginning of this chapter that the time is right to suggest nothing in psychology makes complete sense except in the light of evolution.

While 'Mendel's laws' provide a broad understanding of basic genetics, they have been modified and developed greatly since they were first uncovered (his original article was re-discovered by evolutionists at the beginning of the twentieth century).

THE DEVELOPMENT OF GENETICS SINCE MENDEL

Although Mendel's work was largely ignored during the latter years of the nineteenth century, in 1900 three botanists simultaneously realised the importance of his findings. Hugo DeVries, Carl Correns and Eric von Tschermak, while conducting their own breeding experiments, uncovered Mendel's article and each independently realised that the Monk had discovered the physical foundation of heredity (Pallen 2009). This established Mendel's laws and led to his becoming famous 16 years after his death in 1884. Then during the 1930s it was realised that genes are located on the paired rod-like structures found in the nucleus of each body cell, which are known as **chromosomes**. Today the location of a specific gene on a chromosome is known as a **locus** and alternate genes which can occupy the same locus are known as **alleles**. Humans have 23 such pairs of chromosomes, one of each pair from each parent which provides us with just over 20,000 genes (established by the **Human Genome Project**, Humphrey and Stringer 2019). Combining the new science of genetics with Darwinian selective forces (natural and sexual selection) led to what become known in the twentieth century as **Neo-Darwinism** or the **Modern Evolutionary Synthesis**. Today our understanding of natural selection can be pared down to the simple three-word phrase 'differential gene replication'.

Today we realise that Mendel was extremely fortunate in that the characteristics he studied in pea plants happened to have a very straightforward relationship with inheritance. For one thing, pea colour has a simple dominant/recessive relationship, whereas many characteristics do not have complete dominance (a situation known as **incomplete penetrance**), which means the majority of organisms will show the feature if they have that gene but a small number won't. Some forms of inherited breast cancer show 80 per cent penetrance rates, which means 80 per cent of women with a specific gene will develop this form of breast cancer. Additionally, many characteristics require more than one gene in order to appear; this is a situation where a trait is said to be **polygenic**. Examples of human polygenic traits include height and eye colour. No doubt many cognitive features such as intelligence are also polygenic (Plomin 2018). Finally, one gene can affect more than one trait. This is known as **pleiotropy**. Albinism in humans is a pleiotropic condition as a single gene leads to both pale skin and poor eyesight. Some experts also consider the psychiatric disorder schizophrenia to be pleiotropic because people with psychosis are also often highly creative (see Chapter 6). To complicate matters further, a trait can be both polygenic and pleiotropic! Schizophrenia is most likely a case in point here. These three features of genetics – polygenic, pleiotropic and varying rates of penetrance of genes, mean that, while we still consider Mendelian genetics to be broadly correct, the reality of inheritance of characteristics is frequently more complicated than Mendel had conceptualised.

The discovery of traits that are due to polygenic and pleiotropic genes or that are related to various degrees of penetrance mean that the field of genetics has become far more nuanced and complicated than during the early years of its development. Clearly, when it comes to human behavioural traits and internal states, the relationship between genes and behaviour becomes even more complicated (not to mention controversial). We will consider this further in chapter 4 but at this point we need to gain a greater understanding of what a gene is. The field of genetics took a major step forward (and became even more complicated – see later) following the discovery of the chemical structure of genes, the famous double helix known as deoxyribonucleic acid or **DNA**, by Watson and Crick. This finding led to the development of yet another field of biology known as molecular biology.

THE PHYSICAL STRUCTURE OF GENES: MOLECULAR BIOLOGY

The new science of **molecular biology** began to emerge as soon as Cambridge scientists James Watson and Francis Crick uncovered the structure of DNA in 1953. Molecular biology examines the structure of DNA and other important biological molecules such as proteins. DNA has two main jobs. First, it makes proteins and second, it makes copies of itself. Following Watson and Crick's discovery, a gene came to be defined as a portion of DNA that codes for the production of a large molecule known as a **polypeptide**. A small protein consists of a single polypeptide, but larger ones are made up of a number of polypeptides. Structurally, genes consist of a sequence of units which make up the famous twisted ladder that is the double helix. Each unit of the 'ladder' contains three parts – the outer 'rails' of the ladder which are made up of alternating acid and sugar portions (known together as phosphate deoxyribose) and the inner 'rungs' which consist of one of four different base pairs: **adenine** (A) and **thymine** (T), **cytosine** (C) and **guanine** (G) (see Figure 1.3). A pairs with T and C pairs with G and each rung consists of a base that juts out from each side and makes a weak bond with its partner base. In all, human DNA consists of some 3 billion base pairs. It is these base pairs that code for the production of proteins.

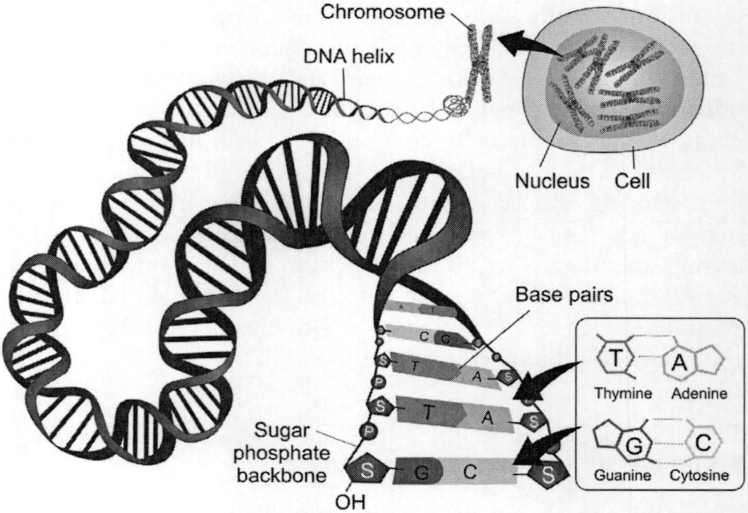

Figure 1.3 The structure of DNA. Note the base pairings that make up the rungs of the ladder and the phosphate deoxyribose rails of the ladder. If stretched out, human DNA would be roughly as long as the average adult human is tall

Given the bonds between these base pairs are relatively weak, this means that, when it is necessary to make a protein, a portion of the DNA can easily unzip, creating two sequences of bases such as GATTACA (which incidentally is the name of a science fiction movie about genetic selection in humans). One of these sequences is then used as a recipe to manufacture a polypeptide and ultimately a protein. (Note in reality protein production requires the gathering together of distributed information from many parts of the chromosome, hence it requires the decoding of many different parts of the DNA molecule rather like the way a computer hard drive takes information spread out from all over the disk to conduct a task.) It is unnecessary for the study of evolutionary psychology to consider the exact molecular biology of the process of protein production (or how DNA makes copies of itself, you may be pleased to know!). Suffice to say, given the **neurones** and **neurotransmitters** (and **receptor sites** for neurotransmitters) of the brain are derived from proteins, knowing this helps us to understand the long-distance relationship between the genes we inherit and our behavioural proclivities and mental states.

GENE EXPRESSION

The proteins that are coded for by our DNA are used in many ways such as enzyme production, regulation of chemical reactions and transportation of substances into and out of cells. For our purposes, however, the most important job that proteins do is to help the formation of the brain and to allow for plasticity of that important organ. Although the brain makes up only 2 per cent of adult body weight, over 30 per cent of genes are devoted to its construction and maintenance. While the vast majority of our body cells contain within them our entire DNA, which parts of this are active (expressed) depends on where they are located and hence the job that they have to do. To put it another way, the level of **gene expression** (activation) depends on where in the body that gene finds itself. To complicate matters further gene expression also depends on what is going on in the environment (see later).

GENES, BRAINS AND BEHAVIOUR

At this point, having introduced the relationship between genes and the brain, it is worth tracing the path from genes to behaviour via the 'middle-man', the brain. As we have mentioned, genes are involved in the formation of the brain. One question we might ask is do genetic differences between people contribute to differences in their brain structure? Broadly speaking the answer is a qualified 'yes'. One way in which people differ due to differences in their genes is via the formation of receptor sites on neurones which are activated (or inhibited) by specific neurotransmitters. There is good evidence to support this, but single genes contribute very little to differences between people. What we have learned in very recent years is that human behavioural traits (and differences in these between people) are related to many differences in genes, in some cases this may be hundreds or even thousands (Plomin, 2018). This means that media headlines suggesting that a 'gene for intelligence' or 'a gene for obesity' has been discovered really means that one gene can be related to quite small differences between people as part of a 'gene-complex'.

It is important to realise that, as with proximate and ultimate levels of explanations for behaviour, we must also consider these two different time frames for the relationship between genes and the brain. Genes influence the organisation and development of the brain both on an evolutionary and within a developmental time-course. In terms of an evolutionary context, over an extremely lengthy period, Darwinian selective pressures (natural and sexual selection) led to the current genetic code for brain development in our species (with slight variations in this code between people). An example of this would be our general species preference for sweet foods. Additionally, during an individual's development their genetic code (or **genome**), through interaction with environmental input, influences brain development, which, in turn, influences behaviour. An example of this might be our early positive experiences with specific sweet foods leading to a preference to seek out certain foods later in life.

It's important also to realise that this book is not largely about the relationship between genes and behaviour, but rather about the relationship between evolutionary forces, current behavioural tendencies and internal states of mind. It is merely necessary that we have some understanding of the relationship between genes and behaviour in as much as genes and brains are the intermediaries between evolution and behaviour.

BOX 1.3 HUMAN EVOLUTION FROM APE TO HUMAN

It is a commonly held belief that humans evolved from chimpanzees. It is, however, more accurate to say that humans and chimpanzees diverged from a common ancestor around seven million years before present (MYBP). The earliest known human-like (***hominin***) species since this split dates back to around six million years and is known as ***Sahelanthropus tchadensis*** (Humphrey and Stringer 2018). Although ***Sahelanthropus*** was very ape-like it did have some early human-like features such as **bipedalism** (walking upright). This was followed around 4.4 MYBP by ***Ardipithecus ramidus*** and then by a number of species of ***Australopithecus*** beginning around 4.2 MYBP. It is likely that a particular species of australopithecine gave rise to the *Homo* line around 2.5 MYBP and via a number of these, in particular ***Homo habilis*** and the ***Homo erectus***, to anatomically modern ***Homo sapiens*** around 150,000 years ago. With each new species, we see more modern human-like features such as shorter arms, a flatter, less jutting face, a more upright posture and a greatly enlarged skull (and hence brain size). We also developed less powerful jaws over this time period (humans have weak jaws compared to the great apes – a chimpanzee could easily bite your finger off!). This apparent journey from ape to human can be deceptive. There are two main myths about human evolution, which we need to dispel. First, there was no preordained passage in this direction but rather a matter of some individuals having better adaptations to various aspects of the savannah once we moved out of the forests (around the time of the *australopithecines*) and therefore producing more surviving offspring. These include problem-solving abilities to capture prey and avoid predators. During the time period we have considered here our brain expanded fourfold. And second, our evolution was not a simple ladder-like process with one more human-like species replacing the previous one. Rather it was much messier than this with, until relatively recent times, a

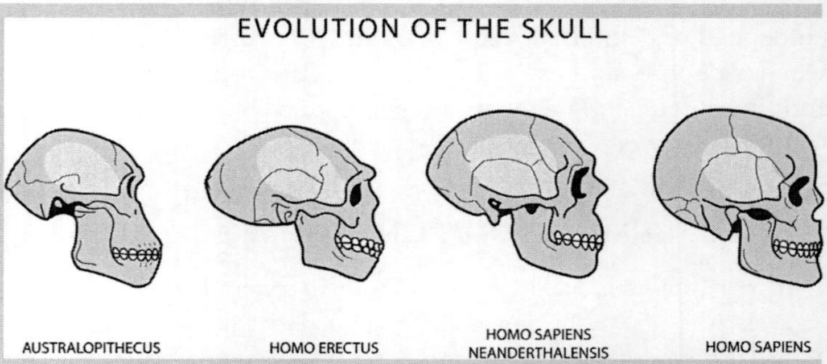

Figure 1.4 Hominin skulls demonstrating increase in cranial capacity

number of hominin species coexisting. Perhaps as many as five or six different species of *homo* and *australopithecines* (also at least two species of *Homo sapiens*, our own ancestors and those of the Neanderthals) coexisted and almost certainly competed for resources with each other, also arguably providing selective pressures that help to form *Homo sapiens* (Figure 1.4 illustrates hominin cranial capacity).

THE DEVELOPMENT OF EVOLUTIONARY PSYCHOLOGY

Having introduced the basic building blocks for an evolutionary approach – Darwin's principles of natural and sexual section and Mendelian genetics – we are now ready to consider the emergence of evolutionary psychology and its major principles. The first of these is the gene's eye view of life.

WHAT DOES NATURAL SELECTION SELECT FOR? DEVELOPING THE GENE'S EYE VIEW

Darwin wrote a great deal about survival of the fittest. But, we might ask, the fittest what? Is it the fittest species, population, group, individual organism, or maybe even the genes within an individual organism? Up until 1960 most people implicitly considered that natural selection arose to aid the survival of the species. This was rarely made explicit, but simply assumed. In the early years of the 1960s one man took the view that the selection pressures operate at the level of the group and in order to support his case he published a book outlining the evidence to support his view. In 1962 Scottish/Canadian biologist Vero Wynne-Edwards published *Animal Dispersion in Relation to Social Behaviour*. In it he argued that, because we see so many examples of altruistic behaviour between members of a group, from insects to apes, then this is evidence that natural selection selects at the level of the group. This appears to make sense. If we think about the alarm calls that many birds make when a predator approaches or the aid meerkats provide for younger members of their clan, or, more extremely, how social insects such as ants and bees lay down their lives to save their hive or nest, then this only appears to make sense if selection acts at the level of the group. Hence, when it comes to altruistic behaviour, **group selection** makes intuitive sense, since animals appear to put aside their individual needs such as breeding for the good of the group. Unfortunately for Wynne-Edwards, some prominent evolutionists immediately spotted a hole in his explanation for **altruism**. In 1964, leading evolutionary biologist John Maynard Smith pointed out that, where members of a group set aside their own selfish needs, there would be strong selective pressure for selfish 'subversion from within'. Imagine, for example, that altruistic members of the group put aside their own selfish needs to produce offspring for the good of the group (as suggested by Wynne-Edwards). A mutant gene that made specific individuals within that group more likely to breed, despite how this might affect the group, would very rapidly out-reproduce the altruistic 'hold back from breeding' individuals within the group. This 'subversion from within' argument was further supported by an American evolutionary biologist by the name of George C. Williams in his 1966 book *Adaptation and Natural Selection*. In it he documented how, when animals make sacrifices for others in their group, it is nearly always for close relatives. Williams also suggested that when animals act in apparently altruistic ways to their own kin they were really helping to promote copies of their own genes in such relatives. This means that such behaviour is not real altruism but ultimately 'selfish'. Williams and Maynard Smith proposed that Darwinian selection occurs at the level of 'genes or individuals'. Their arguments were based both on theoretical grounds and on recently published work by another evolutionary biologist, William Hamilton.

KIN-SELECTION: HAMILTON'S RULE SOLVED THE 'ANT PROBLEM'

Williams and Maynard-Smith countered Wynne-Edwards' group selection by arguing that apparent altruistic behaviour, rather than evolving to aid the group, was in reality a case of relatives supporting each other. This raises the question why do relatives support each other? While parent-to-offspring aid is common and what we would naturally expect, Williams and Maynard Smith argued that we can also expect to see apparent altruism towards other relatives. In order to make this argument they drew on observational and theoretical work of Cambridge biologist William Hamilton. Hamilton (1964) studied the social behaviour of ants and wondered himself, not only why they often sacrificed themselves for their nestmates, but also how it was that sterile worker ants might have arisen, given these females don't breed but rather leave this to the queen? Hamilton solved this problem when he realised that, due to their particular method of breeding, these sterile worker ants share 75 per cent of their genes with their sisters. Hamilton then began to consider a 'gene's eye view' of natural selection, and immediately realised such non-queen worker ants could actually pass on a larger proportion of their genes indirectly by, instead of breeding themselves, helping to raise their younger sisters. For each sister raised, they are passing on 75 per cent of their genes rather than the 50 per cent that would be passed on via normal sexual reproduction. To Hamilton, ant colonies should really be perceived as a form of extended family where the genetic interests of all are served by the apparent altruistic behaviour of some. He then went on to make history in behavioural biology by extending this argument to other species and suggesting self-sacrificing behaviour towards others is more likely to be 'selected for' the greater the number of their genes two individuals share by common descent. In this way he shifted the emphasis from the group to the individual and from the individual to the gene. John Maynard Smith called this new way of looking at selective forces **kin selection** in as much as our relatives are involved in this part of natural selection.

Since he first proposed it, Hamilton's hypothesis has been developed into **inclusive fitness** theory, a concept that was to become one of the foundation stones of evolutionary psychology. Inclusive fitness consists of the number of copies of their genes an individual passes on to future generations and includes both genes passed directly via offspring produced and indirectly by giving aid to other 'non-direct' kin. These are often younger kin such as nephews and nieces who are less likely to survive without aid. In such cases, while direct offspring share 50 per cent of their genes with each parent, 25 per cent are also shared with uncles and aunts. Note that the proportion of genes shared between two relatives by common descent is known as the **coefficient of relatedness** which is represented as 'r'. So, if an animal is not in a position to breed itself it can still pass on a fair proportion of its genes by providing aid to such kin. This value varies from 1 (identical twins who shares 100 per cent of their genes by common descent) to 0 (non-relative who shares no genes by common descent). Hence in theory we can all work out our inclusive fitness by adding up the 'r's for each offspring produced (each with an 'r' of 0.5) and other relatives that we provide aid to (each of which is weighted by its 'r' such as nephews with 0.25 and cousins with 0.125). Hamilton produced a formula which specifies the conditions under which an individual is likely to show altruistic behaviour to kin: $rB > C$. Here r is the proportion of genes shared, B is the benefit gained by the recipient and C is the cost to the altruist. Translating this equation into prose we can say that altruistic behaviour can be predicted if the benefit to the recipient is greater than the cost to the altruist factoring in the proportion of genes shared between the altruist and the recipient of the aid. Hence, we are more likely to act to aid a sibling ($r = 0.5$) than a nephew ($r = 0.25$) and more likely to provide aid to a nephew than a cousin ($r = 0.125$). This equation, which has become known as 'Hamilton's rule', has helped researchers to understand and predict when altruism is likely to occur in social animals and appears to stand up well to scrutiny, both in ourselves and in other species (Dunbar 2021). Today evolutionists make use of inclusive fitness theory to help understand many instances of altruism such as why meerkats aid youngsters who are not necessarily their direct offspring, and why Florida scrub jays help to raise their younger siblings. It also helps us to understand why adult wild dogs of Africa regurgitate meat from a kill for other members of the pack. In all of these cases it has been shown that individuals pass on their genes by helping relatives of various degrees of kinship. Moreover, the chance of engaging in altruistic behaviour increases, as does the proportion of genes shared. Hence the self-sacrificing behaviour of social insects such as ants is simply an extreme example of Hamilton's rule.

RECIPROCAL ALTRUISM: ROBERT TRIVERS AND MUTUAL BACK SCRATCHING

There are of course limits to how far we can push kin selection theory as an explanation for all of the altruistic behaviour observed. Examples exist in the animal kingdom where aid is provided to non-relatives. These include, for example, many non-kin birds and primates which aid each other despite sharing no genes by common descent (Colquhoun et al. 2020). The explanation for this form of altruism was uncovered by a young Harvard biologist by the name of Robert Trivers.

In 1971 Trivers published his first research article in which he outlined a way in which unrelated individuals of social species can provide aid to each other within an evolutionary framework. In so doing he introduced a new concept into evolutionary biology, which he called **reciprocal altruism**. In a nutshell, reciprocal altruism can occur when the benefit to the recipient is greater than the cost to the altruist, then, as long as a similar degree of aid is later reciprocated, both the parties benefit, and such behaviour can be selected for. We will examine this concept further when we consider social and moral behaviour in Chapter 3. Suffice to say here that the concept of reciprocal altruism (or simply 'reciprocation') has become an important one for those interested in the relationship between evolution and behaviour; particularly so for our own species (Colquhoun et al. 2020).

DAWKINS' SELFISH GENE: SPELLING OUT THE GENE'S EYE VIEW

Throughout the 1960s the concepts of reciprocal altruism, kin selection and inclusive fitness theory began to have a growing influence on behavioural biologists. Then in 1976 British evolutionary biologist Richard Dawkins brought the ideas of Hamilton, Trivers, Maynard Smith and Williams to a much wider audience when he published *The Selfish Gene*. In addition to biologists interested in animal behaviour, *The Selfish Gene* also came to be read by psychologists and by a fair proportion of the general reading public. It made use of Hamilton and other evolutionary theorist's view of why animals (and humans) demonstrate both selfish and apparent altruistic behaviour towards others by taking the gene's eye view of social behaviour.

BOX 1.4 ARE WE STILL EVOLVING?

Until relatively recently, most experts have thought that human evolution had slowed down possibly to the point of stopping. Indeed, many biological and social scientists assumed biological evolution had given way to cultural evolution. The reason for this mindset is because, while other species populations adapt to changes in their environment, human populations have achieved a fair degree of control over their environment (especially since we developed agriculture between 10,000 and 12,000 years ago); therefore, logically we might predict evolution must now be very slow (if it takes place at all) for our species? Counterintuitively, however, it appears that humans have continued to evolve over the last 10,000 years. We know this, due to advances in our ability to read the human genome and develop large DNA data banks (Stock, 2008). What molecular biologists have done in recent years is to study lengthy stretches of DNA to determine the number of common 'blocks' of base-pairs (see earlier) that appear in samples. When molecular biologists see the same lengthy genetic sequence in 20 per cent of a large sample this suggests natural selection has been active in 'recent' years (within 1000 to 10,000 years). In carrying out such studies of the genome, evolutionists have reached the conclusion that, not only are we still evolving, but the rate of evolution is actually speeding up. This raises two questions. First, what sort of evolutionary changes have we undergone and second what is causing this rapid evolution? With regard to the first question, examples of evolutionary changes include many sub-populations developing the ability to digest cow's milk since we started to herd cattle and the evolution of blue eye colour in northern populations. More importantly, some experts have also suggested we have improved in our social intelligence abilities (Dunbar 2021). With regard to the second question, one reason is simply due to sheer numbers. Large numbers speed up the rate of evolution because a larger number of **mutations** and gene combinations emerge for natural selection to work on. This means that a large number of adaptations to environmental challenges can evolve more rapidly. Human populations have grown enormously over the last 10,000 years. Ten thousand years ago there were around 10 million of us. Today there are 7.7 billion of us (an 800-fold increase). This, of course, meant we came into contact with larger numbers of people which, in turn, increased selective pressures to develop more complex forms of social communication. This leads us on to the second reason we are still evolving. When more complex forms of social communication develop, then this changes selection pressures (Dunbar 2014; 2021). Such changes are speeding up. Two generations ago people did not own PCs and one generation ago they did not have Smartphones. Hence, we are changing aspects of social communication rapidly and this may currently be altering selection pressures. Smartphones might not make us smarter, but they certainly alter the ways in which we communicate with each other and this, in turn, may ultimately change our evolutionary trajectory (Workman 2020).

In *The Selfish Gene* Dawkins introduced the concept of the gene's eye view to a wider audience and in order to do this he distinguished between two types of biological entity, 'vehicles' and 'replicators'. Vehicles is the name he gave to organisms while replicators are the genes that build organisms and then arrange to have themselves passed on to new vehicles. Hence, if we think back to the peppered moth's adaptation, those replicators that produced the more appropriate markings in their vehicles were more likely to continue down the generations, provided the environment did not change once more. For Dawkins, we should focus on what is in it for the replicators if we want to understand how evolution works because these are the biological entities that endure over an evolutionary timescale (hence the concept of the

Figure 1.5 Author of *The Selfish Gene*, Richard Dawkins

gene's eye view). In contrast, us vehicles are mere transient beings built by the replicators to make copies of said replicators. In this way, Dawkins' genes-eye view is the one we should focus on if we really wish to understand how evolution works.

Unbeknown to Dawkins, at the same time as he was writing *The Selfish Gene*, a North American evolutionist by the name of E. O. Wilson was also developing broadly similar ideas and committing them to print. In 1975 Wilson published *Sociobiology: The New Synthesis*. Sociobiology also focussed on the ideas of Hamilton and the other aforementioned evolutionists to suggest that, in order understand behaviour we need to view it as the product of evolutionary forces. You may recall that this means asking ultimate why questions about behaviour. Although the term **sociobiology** had been used occasionally since the 1940s, it immediately became associated with Wilson. Wilson's view was slightly different from Dawkins' in as much as it was less focussed on genes/replicators but similar in that he saw our and other species' behaviour as having evolved to make us inclusive fitness maximisers. *Sociobiology* also differed from *The Selfish Gene* in that, whereas the latter caused a degree of debate among evolutionary biologists, the former caused a furore not only in biology but also in the social sciences (and among some psychologists). This may well be due, in part, to the fact that, unlike Dawkins, Wilson made explicit that he was discussing human behaviour in his final chapter. Moreover, he suggested *Sociobiology* would 'cannibalise' the social sciences, suggesting that ways of explaining human behaviour that did not incorporate evolutionary principals would become redundant.

Many behavioural biologists (and some psychologists) who had followed the developments in the relationship between evolution and behaviour that occurred between the early 1960s and the 1970s were stirred into action and the field of sociobiology became one of very active research. It looked at this point in the late 1970s and early 1980s as if Darwin's prediction that 'psychology will be based on a new foundation' was being fulfilled. Unfortunately, there was a fly in the ointment. Wilson, it appears, had overstepped the mark and social scientists (and some psychologists and even biologists) fought back. They suggested behavioural responses such as aggression can better be explained by the social environment than by biological factors (Segerstråle 2000). Some of the criticisms were personally aimed at Wilson and, although he reassured his critics that he had always considered behaviour to be the outcome of complex interactions between genes and environment, the damage was done. To many, sociobiology took on negative connotations and many biologists preferred the label **behavioural ecologist** (a broadly synonymous term which had been developing over the same time period). Today the term sociobiology is used less frequently than in the latter years of the twentieth century, despite the fact that much important research was published under that umbrella term (some journals have even changed their names to exclude the term sociobiology).

FROM SOCIOBIOLOGY AND BEHAVIOURAL ECOLOGY TO EVOLUTIONARY PSYCHOLOGY

Despite the misgivings of (or perhaps because of) some social and natural scientists, a new approach to understanding human behaviour within an evolutionary context rapidly emerged. The term 'evolutionary psychology' was first used by American biologist Michael Ghisenlin in an article published in 1973 (note this was prior to Wilson's *Sociobiology* and Dawkins' *The Selfish Gene*). Ghisenlin's use of the term was, however, quite different to modern day interpretations of evolutionary psychology and, although the term was occasionally used during the 1970s and 1980s, it came into common use following the publication of a 1992 multi-authored book entitled *The Adapted Mind: Evolutionary Psychology and the Generation of Culture* by North American trio Jerome Barkow, Leda Cosmides and John Tooby (Barkow, Cosmides and Tooby 1992; Workman and Taylor 2021). So, we might ask how does evolutionary psychology differ from sociobiology (and behavioural ecology)? Although evolutionary psychology draws on the developments in evolutionary theory that have been outlined earlier, Barkow, Cosmides and Tooby suggested it differs from earlier approaches in two ways. First, the main emphasis is on psychological mechanisms – although these are often interpreted from behavioural responses. Second, it does not suggest, unlike sociobiology, that humans are currently fitness maximisers, but rather that we have adaptations that would most likely have helped to boost inclusive fitness during the ancient past. Many of these responses and internal states are not considered to be fitness maximising today, due to the fact that we no longer live in the environment in which we evolved. In their words, 'much of post-Pleistocene society is *evolutionary unanticipated*'. That is, there is a mismatch between the environment in which our species evolved and the current environment (the **mismatch hypothesis**). This, in turn, can often lead to maladaptive behaviour today because there is a mismatch between the environment in which we evolved (the Pleistocene) and the environment we live in now (see Chapter 6). This is considered to be the case because we have altered our environment much faster than natural selection allows for emotional, motivational and cognitive changes to occur (although it is now known evolutionary change can be more rapid than was thought back in 1992 – see 'Are we still evolving' above). Our current tendency to gravitation towards ancestral adaptations may even mean that aspects of our environment can be maladaptive for many today. An example of this is our evolved desire for sugar, fat and salt which, given how widely available these are now, frequently leads to high levels of obesity, diabetes and coronary heart disease (at least in industrialised nations). Since the time of Barkow, Cosmides and Tooby, evolutionary psychologists have concentrated largely on our evolved psychological mechanisms. This does not mean that internal states or behavioural responses are hard-wired but rather that we are motivated to find learning experiences positive that would have had fitness benefits for our ancient ancestors. In the words of Jerome Barkow:

> Evolutionary psychologists argue that our shared evolved mechanisms make for the psychic unity of our species, our human nature.
>
> (Barkow 2006, p. 27)

Another concept that Barkow, Cosmides and Tooby drew on was Bowlby's (1969) 'environment of evolutionary adaptedness' or EEA. While the EEA for our species has been related to the Pleistocene, it is important to realise that it is more than simply a time period, but rather describes the time, place(s) and selection pressures that led to the evolution of a species (including humans; Workman, Taylor and Barkow 2022). Despite being a controversial concept (Barkow himself prefers 'environments of evolutionary adaptedness' or EEAs today), it is certainly helpful to consider these selective challenges that our ancestors faced during the Pleistocene (and over the last 11,000 years), if we want to understand modern psychological mechanisms.

Although this approach has not escaped criticism (we will consider criticism of the field at various points throughout), such disapproval has been less frequent and less extreme than its predecessor, sociobiology, and the field has gained a high level of academic (and public) acceptance over the last 30 years. Today evolutionary psychology has been used to explore ultimate explanations for virtually all aspects of human behaviour from the development of language and morality through evolved emotional and cognitive mechanisms to why people differ and why we see cultural diversity. These are the themes we explore in future chapters.

Most of this chapter has been concerned with understanding the relationship between Darwin's theory of natural selection and behaviour. In the next chapter we turn to his second theory for evolutionary change – sexual selection and how this is considered by evolutionary psychologists to have shaped differences in behaviour between the sexes.

SUMMARY

Evolutionary psychologists make use of ultimate explanations to help understand the human condition. Ultimate explanations consider the evolutionary forces that shaped a species' behavioural repertoire and internal states. This stands in contrast to traditional psychological approaches, which consider proximate (here-and-now) levels of explanation. Darwin fleshed out his theory of evolution by natural selection in 1859, followed by his concept of sexual selection in 1871. Whereas in natural selection, the forces of nature do the selecting, in sexual selection the opposite sex does the selecting. Mendelian genetics was re-discovered and developed at the beginning of the twentieth century. Mendel outlined three laws of inheritance: characteristics are coded for by paired genes which can be dominant or recessive; it is possible for two individuals to have different genotypes (their genetic code) but still have the same phenotype (characteristics); genes are particulate and passed on intact rather than blending. Combining genetics with Darwinism led to the development of Neo-Darwinism or the Modern Evolutionary Synthesis during the twentieth century. Following the discovery of the chemical structure of genes (DNA) the new field of molecular biology developed. DNA codes for protein production. Many of these proteins are involved in brain and nervous system development which helps to explain why differences between people can, in part, be explained by differences in their genetic code. Fossil and genetic evidence suggests human and chimp ancestors split from a common ancestor around seven million years before present (YBP). Anatomically, modern *Homo sapiens* arose from *Homo erectus* around 150,000 years YBP. Although Darwin, in effect, proposed the development of evolutionary psychology in 1859, it only began to emerge in the late twentieth century. Important concepts in evolutionary psychology include William Hamilton's kin-selection, where animals favour those who share the greatest proportion of their genes by common descent, and Robert Trivers' concept of reciprocation where organisms provide aid in the 'expectation' that this will be reciprocated at a later time. The proportion of an organism's genes passed on either directly through offspring or via other non-descendent relatives is known as their inclusive fitness. While E. O. Wilson's *Sociobiology* and Richard Dawkins' *The Selfish Gene* helped to initiate the ultimate, evolutionary level of explanation for human behaviour during the 1970s, most experts trace the development of evolutionary psychology as a discipline back to the publication in 1992 of *The Adapted Mind: Evolutionary Psychology and the Generation of Culture* edited by Jerome Barkow, Leda Cosmides and John Tooby. Today evolutionary psychology is concerned with understanding our species' shared evolved mechanisms which would most likely have boosted our inclusive fitness in the context of ancient recurrent challenges and opportunities.

FURTHER READING

Buss, D. M. (2019) *Evolutionary Psychology: The New Science of the Mind*(6th edn). New York: Routledge.

Dunbar, R. I. M. (2021) *Friends: Understanding the Power of our Most Important Relationships*. Boston, MA: Little Brown.

Humphrey, L. and Stringer, C. (2019) *Our Human Story*. London: Natural History Museum.

Pallen, M. (2009) *The Rough Guide to Evolution*. London: Penguin.

Plomin, R. (2018) *Blueprint: How DNA Makes Us Who We Are*. London: Allen Lane/Penguin Books.

Workman, L., Reader, W. and Barkow, J. H. (Eds) (2020) *Cambridge Handbook of Evolutionary Perspectives on Human Behavior*. Cambridge: Cambridge University Press.

2

SEXUAL SELECTION AND MATE CHOICE

SEXUAL SELECTION: DARWIN'S SECOND SELECTIVE FORCE

In Chapter 1 we saw how Darwin's main selective force, natural selection, has become the accepted mechanism for adaptive evolutionary change. This concept of survival of the fittest is however pointless unless the 'fittest' pass on their genes that code for characteristics which enhanced their survival. If an individual from a sexually reproducing species is to pass on its genes, then it will need to compete for the attentions of the opposite sex. Note that 'competing for the attentions of' implies both competition with your own sex and impressing the other sex. Hence, while some animal characteristics have evolved to aid survival, others may have arisen to boost competitive ability and level of attractiveness. Darwin realised this and, in 1871 in his book *The Descent of Man and Selection in Relation to Sex*, he developed the concept of a second selective force, which he called 'sexual selection'. **Sexual selection** has two components, **intrasexual selection**, which is competition between members of one sex and **intersexual selection**, which is impressing the opposite sex. One question we might ask is, how exactly does sexual selection differ from natural selection? As we outlined in Chapter 1, the essential difference is that, while in natural selection the forces of nature act as the 'selector', in sexual selection the opposite sex takes on this role. It's important to realise that while natural selection drives the sexes in the same direction, sexual selection can drive them in different directions. This means that where we see differences in form and behaviour between the sexes, we can generally trace this back to

DOI: 10.4324/9780429274428-2

sexual selection. For other species this explanation for sex differences is uncontroversial; but when it comes to our own species, the concept of evolved differences between men and women is a contentious one for many social scientists.

In this chapter we consider the effects of sexual selection on other species before examining its effects on humans. Before doing this, however, we first have to solve a riddle that most people never even consider. Why do we reproduce sexually?

WHY SEX?

There's a problem with sex. According to modern evolutionary theory, natural selection selects for those individuals which can pass

Figure 2.1 Charles Darwin in old age

on the largest proportion of their genes to future generations; that is, those best able to boost their inclusive fitness. In the case of species that breed asexually, such as many single-celled organisms and even some multi-celled ones, cloning identical copies of themselves means that each offspring receives 100 per cent of its single parent's genes. Hence, when say an amoeba survives to produce five 'offspring' (via binary fission whereby it simply splits into two when it reaches a certain size), then it has passed on 500 per cent of its genes. Now compare this with an individual from a sexually reproducing species. Here, two individuals form gametes (sex cells – sperm and ova) by halving the number of genes in each sex cell. They then combine these two gametes (i.e. have sex) to form a **zygote** (or fertilised egg) which eventually, all being well, develops into a new individual. Note that, in order to reproduce, each individual throws away half of its genes. This means that, in order to pass on 500 per cent of their genes, each sexually reproducing individual must produce ten surviving offspring. Bearing in mind the fact that early on in organic evolutionary history all species reproduced asexually, then sexual reproduction must be twice as good as asexual reproduction if it is to replace it in a species. (It is worth pointing out that in addition to this cost there are two others, the cost of producing males who do not go on to reproduce and the cost associated with the efforts of courtship. Both of these, however, pale into insignificance in comparison to throwing half of your genes away). Hence, in a nutshell, the main problem with sex is, how can we explain why such a form of reproduction evolved when in competition with asexual reproduction? Incidentally, the fact that there is a problem with sexual reproduction was only realised once genetics had become a well-developed science in the second half of the twentieth century (Maynard Smith 1978; Williams 1975).

So far, we have established the fact that, if sex is to evolve in a species, then it must provide individuals that make use of it with an advantage that it is at least twice as good as sex. We have not, however, established what that advantage is. During the 1990s one of the authors of this book asked the famous evolutionist John Maynard Smith if biologists had worked out the answer to this conundrum. He replied, 'oh yes we have several answers, we just don't know which one is correct!'. It would be beyond the scope of this book to examine in detail all of the theories that have been developed to explain sex but here is a brief synopsis of the history and current thinking on this matter.

American evolutionary biologist George Williams suggested in 1975 that sexual reproduction functions like a raffle whereby each offspring can be likened to a ticket which has a different number on it. With asexual reproduction each offspring, being genetically identical, is equivalent to having lots of raffle tickets with the same number. Once you introduce sex into the equation, however, you create variation in the number on each ticket. In this way, for parents, given an unpredictable future environment, more of your offspring are likely to win the raffle than if they all had the same number on them (i.e. the same set of genes). While some evolutionists have argued over the utility of the raffle analogy, most today agree that the variation sex provides has to be a major part of the answer. Another suggestion put forward in 1973 by Norwegian biologist Leigh Van Valen is known as the **Red Queen** hypothesis (See Ridley 1993). According to this hypothesis, multi-celled organisms are locked into a 'host–parasite **arms race**' in which each side of the equation tries to gain an advantage. Pathogens such as viruses and bacteria appear to evolve very rapidly compared to longer lived organisms such as mammals. This is due largely to having such a brief generation time and because there are so many of them that fortuitous mutations on the pathogen's side can spread very rapidly and tip the balance in their favour. (Note that by 'fortuitous' we mean they are better able to invade their hosts – think of the devastating infection rates of the COVID-19 virus following mutation). The way the host species responds is through sex which creates variety in offspring and means that some are more likely to develop immunity more rapidly. Incidentally, this hypothesis is called the Red Queen because in *Alice through the Looking Glass* by Lewis Carroll, when Alice notices they are running but not getting anywhere, she is told by the Red Queen, in wonderland 'it takes all of the running you can do to stay in the same place'. Hence, pathogen and host are both constantly 'running' to keep up with each other's counter-adaptations.

To cut a long story short, today most evolutionists consider that sexual reproduction arose due to the advantages it provides through increasing genetic variation. When you think about it, asexual reproduction leads to identical offspring and, bar the odd mutation, no variation in offspring. This means that pathogens which take out one of your offspring will likely take all of them out. Hence sex, which brings a variety of genes together, leads to variation that most likely provides at least some of your offspring with greater resistance to a given pathogen.

Evidence to support this view includes the observation that, in species that can reproduce both asexually or sexually, when parasite load is high, individuals tend to shift from the former to the latter (Hamilton, Axelrod and Tanese 1990).

SEXUAL SELECTION AND PARENTAL INVESTMENT THEORY

By developing sexual selection theory Darwin was able to explain why, throughout the animal kingdom, males and females differ so much from each other. Because of competition for females, males tend to be larger and, in many species, they have a lower threshold for aggression. Just think of the difference between bulls and cows or stags and does. In both species males have better developed horns and, at least during the breeding season, a lower threshold for aggression. In addition to this competition, males also have to attract females and convince them to mate with them. Hence, the elaborate train of the peacock compared to the relatively plain peahen. In a sense, while we can think of natural selection as driving the sexes in the same direction, sexual selection teases them apart. The only problem Darwin had with the concept of sexual selection is that he never really managed to explain why it is generally this way around. Why should males be the competitive sex? Why should males be the sexy ones constantly vying for female attention? And why should females be the choosy ones?

It was to be a century after Darwin's original work on sexual selection that a young American evolutionist by the name of Robert Trivers finally developed a full explanation. In 1972 Trivers suggested that males attempt to impress females (intrasexual selection) because the latter generally invest a great deal more in the production of offspring than the former. Think about it. Even in humans where there is some male aid in raising offspring, the female still has the costs of gestation and milk production (in the vast majority of mammals all the males provide is sperm). In birds, females produce highly costly eggs and spend a great deal of time

Figure 2.2 Peacock showing his feathers to peahen, who appears to look unimpressed

incubating and feeding the offspring (in songbirds most males do help out at the nest but again they do not, of course, have the enormous cost of egg production). In Trivers' view, males compete for females because, in effect, females bring huge resources to the production of offspring. Trivers called the efforts each sex put into offspring production **parental investment**. Hence, it is this asymmetry in parental investment that helps to explain why males are competitive and females are choosy about whom they mate with. A male that is fit enough to produce colourful plumage or huge body size is signalling they are a good bet to recombine their genes with. Currently it is believed that choosy ancestral females led to the evolution of sexy competitive males today.

Put formally, Trivers defined parental investment as:

> [A]ny investment by a parent in an offspring that increases the chances that offspring will survive at the expense of the parent's ability to invest in any other offspring.
>
> (Trivers 1972, p. 139)

BOX 2.1 SEXUAL SELECTION AND BIPARENTAL CARE IN HUMAN EVOLUTION

Although in some species of lesser apes such as the agile gibbon we observe males helping to raise offspring, amongst the great apes, male parental care is not observed. In contrast, **biparental care** is commonly observed across all human societies. Why, we might ask is this the case in our species and what effect has biparental care had on human evolution?

Fossil evidence shows that brain size has increased fourfold over the last four million years. Interestingly, this has also been a period where the pelvic girdle has narrowed to allow for improvements in bipedal locomotion. Clearly, giving birth to an increasingly large-headed baby through a narrowing pelvic girdle presented our female ancestors with a bit of a headache. So how did evolution solve this problem? Today evolutionists consider that selective pressures led to our female ancestors delivering the foetus at an earlier stage in development. This means that hominin babies were born at an increasingly dependent state in comparison with other primates. This, in turn, meant that biparental care made sense for all parties. Hence, we can trace biparental care back to the challenges and opportunities provided by bipedal locomotion combined with an increase in brain size.

This increase in male parental investment almost certainly influenced the behaviour of both sexes (as this is observed in other species). One change is that, once males are investing in offspring, they also become choosy about their partners, at least for long-term relationships. It also means that females become more competitive for such male investment. During the last 20 years a number of evolutionary psychologists have suggested that, following the emergence of biparental care in our species, the main driving force for the evolution of intelligence shifted from natural to sexual selection.

American evolutionist Geoffrey Miller calls this the **mating mind hypothesis** and proposed that, as an increasingly dependent offspring was being born into a demanding savannah environment, it paid both males and females to mate with and form a pair-bond with bright, caring individuals (Miller 2000). This, in turn, led to ancestral members of our species becoming significantly more intelligent than other primates and helps to explain why our brain has quadrupled in size during human evolution (Workman 2016).

Note we stated above that females 'generally' invest more in offspring than males. In fact, while this is the case for the vast majority of animal species, there are cases where the situation is revered. If we consider a North American shore bird known as the jacana, we see sex role reversal with males providing nearly all of the incubation and subsequent feeding of chicks, and we observe that they are smaller and less aggressive than their female counterparts. For their part, the more brightly coloured female jacanas (also known as 'lily trotters'), compete for the attentions of other males by acting aggressively towards other females. Each female mates with a number of males and maintains a 'harem' of several males. Each of the males attends a specific nest which floats on vegetation such as water lilies. This system of one female to a number of male mates is known as **polyandry** and is rare in comparison to the reverse **polygyny** (one male to a number of females) system. Note this finding of larger, more dominant females where males invest more in the production of offspring is a good test for Trivers' parental investment theory as he stated the sex which invests the least will compete for the sex which invests the most without specifying which sex falls into each category. Since, in jacanas males invest more highly it's not surprising that they are smaller than the females and that females compete for their attentions (Emlen and Wrege 2004a, 2004b). This sex role reversal, while rare, also occurs in other species of birds and, interestingly, in seahorses, where the males incubate up to a thousand young in a special brood pouch. In fact, this pouch has recently been found to provide nutrients for the developing young making it arguably equivalent to pregnancy in female placental mammals (Skalkos, et al. 2020). In contrast to these exceptions the minimum obligatory parental investment is much higher for the vast majority of female animals.

FEMALE CHOICE: DID DARWIN GET IT RIGHT?

During the nineteenth century, while most biologists accepted Darwin's concept of male/male competition being a driving force for evolutionary change, the vast majority rejected the notion of female choice as also leading to evolved differences between the sexes. The prevailing view was that animals simply did not have the intellectual ability to discriminate between mates of differing quality. Moreover, even if females did have this ability, given that males are generally larger than females, surely the 'weaker sex' had little control over whom they mated with? Even Darwin's contemporary (and co-discoverer of natural selection) Alfred Russel Wallace, argued that, for female choice of male quality to work, it would require the latter to have a sense of aesthetics comparable to humans (Zuc and Simmons 2018). Although Darwin made it clear he considered the way that female choice operated may vary quite considerably between species, the early criticisms stuck, and the concept of female choice was largely ignored for the remainder of the nineteenth and much of the twentieth century. In fact, it's fair to say that, with one or two exceptions, all aspects of sexual selection were omitted from studies of the relationship between evolution and behaviour until the latter years of the last century. Hence for around one hundred years following the publication of *The Descent of Man and Selection in Relation to Sex* females were perceived by evolutionists as passive and acquiescent in matters of mate choice. How wrong they were.

BOX 2.2 IS RED PERCEIVED AS DOMINANT IN HUMAN MALES?

It is now well established that red colouration is a sign of male quality in many animal species. One question we might ask is, is it possible that this might also be the case in our own species? We know that anger leads to a reddening of the face while fear often leads to a pale pallor. But does this translate to dominance and

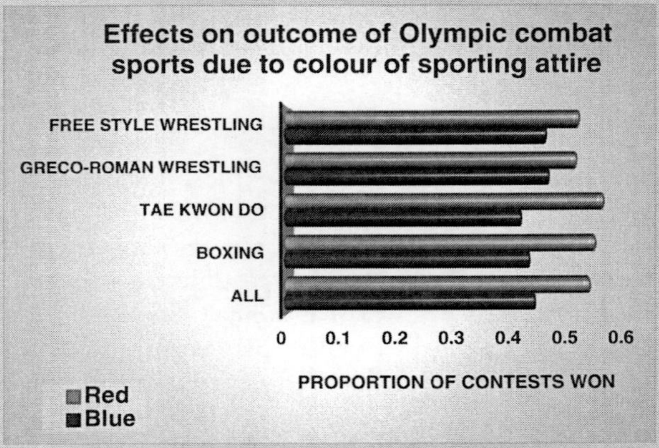

Figure 2.3 Influence of colour of sporting attire on the outcome of Olympic combat sports (based on Hill and Barton 2005)

submissive behaviour? Russel Hill and Robert Barton from the University of Durham came up with a novel way to test this. They noted that in Olympic combat sports combatants are randomly allocated either red or blue outfits. They postulated that those allocated red might have an advantage simply because they are wearing that colour. In analysing all of the combat sport that men took part in: boxing, tae kwon do, Greco-Roman wrestling and free style wrestling from during the 2004 Olympic games, they found male competitors wearing red outfits won significantly more competitions than those wearing blue. Note that in the bar graph in Figure 2.3, if wins were randomly distributed, we would expect to see a 0.50 win rate; but in all four sports red won significantly more times than blue. Perhaps we have retained a primate heritage of perceiving red as a dominant hue?

WHAT DO FEMALES WANT?

Over the last 40 years evidence for female choice and its effects on the males of a species has grown rapidly. In fact, female choice has been observed throughout the animal kingdom from frogs to birds to elephant seals to deer and in many species of primate. To name but a few. But what, we might ask, do females want? Which male features are most likely to lead them to accept a male's advances? In our closest relatives, the primates, there is clear evidence that females chose males considered to be physically attractive and to have status within the group. In many species of primate, bright colours are associated with status. These include vervet monkeys, gelada baboons (see Figure 2.6), mandrills and rhesus macaques (Clutton-Brock and McAuliffe 2009). Both observational and experimental evidence suggests such bright colouration is favoured by females and this, in turn, leads to an increase in colour differentiation between males and females over many generations. You may have noticed in wildlife programmes on TV that some monkeys have particularly red faces (and that your eye is drawn to these individuals). If you have, then you have been focussing on males of high rank within the group. Interestingly, in the wild, female monkeys spend more time grooming and generally paying attention to those males with a redder complexion (Clutton-Brock and McAuliffe 2009). In fact, in many species, males of high rank have noticeably redder faces than lower ranking individuals. This is particularly true of rhesus macaques. In one study the investigators manipulated pictures of male rhesus macaques and allowed females to view them. The females spent far longer attending to the redder faced males than the paler ones (Waitt et al. 2003). Moreover, red colouration is favoured by females of many species outside of primates and appears to be a sexually selected testosterone-dependent sign of dominance in male animals (Clutton-Brock and McAuliffe, 2009).

Colour is not of course the only signal of status or attraction that females favour. In many avian species females appear to choose males with the longest, most elaborate tail feathers. A classic example of this is the African widowbird. This species, which is found in Kenya, is polygynous, with the more elaborately plumaged males maintaining territories into which they attempt to coax females to mate with them. Once each female has mated with a male, she then builds a nest in his territory and subsequently lays her eggs into it. The male widowbird's attempts to attract females into their territories consists of repeatedly leaping up above the long grass and displaying their extremely long tail feathers (approximately 50 cm). In the early 1980s Swedish zoologist Malte Andersson suspected that females based their choices of whom to mate with on the basis of the length of the male's tail. In order to test this, Andersson experimentally manipulated the tail length of a series of male birds to form groups of long (75 cm) and short tail (14 cm) length (plus two control groups – group 1 with the tail cut and glued back the same size and group 2 – an unaltered group). This involved the shortening and lengthening of various males' tails (through use of superglue and scissors). He then compared the number of nests prior to and following these changes in length. The results were pretty clear-cut as females were seen to prefer to nest in the long-tailed males' territories by a ratio of 4:1 when compared with the short-tailed males (see Figure 2.4).

HUMAN MATE CHOICE PREFERENCES AND SEX DIFFERENCES IN BEHAVIOUR

You may at this point be wondering what the tail length of the African widowbird or the red faces of many male primates has to do with human reproductive behaviour? The answer is quite a lot

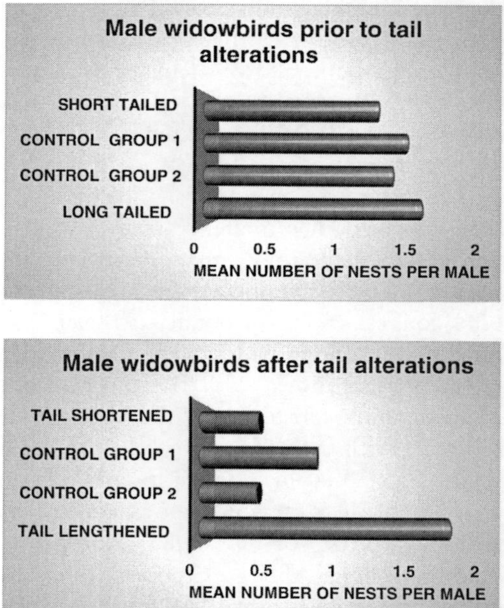

Figure 2.4 Average number of nests in each male widowbird's territory in relation to tail length (prior to and following alteration, based on Andersson 1982)

actually. Much of the theoretical and empirical work on human sex differences has been built on the work of animal behavioural ecologists. Having observed the degree to which parental investment theory works in other species, over the last 30 years evolutionary psychologists have made use of insights from animal studies to test hypotheses about human behaviour. According to evolutionists, because ancestral males and females, for the most part, faced identical challenges during the EEA such as avoiding predators and pathogens, and finding suitable places to forage and shelter, we should have evolved similar adaptations. However, our male and female ancestors faced different challenges, those that are involved in reproductive behaviour. Females had to be able to complete gestation, parturition and lactate successfully. They also had to ensure males would make for appropriate mates to support them in such reproductive phases. Males, for their part, had to find fertile females, convince them to become a mate and then ensure any offspring produced by said mate was theirs rather than another man's. Evolutionary psychologists propose that it is due to these differing ancient recurrent reproductive requirements, that we see some differences between the sexes in current psychological make-up. The view has become known as **sexual strategies theory**, a term coined by two premiant evolutionary psychologists, David Buss and his co-researcher David Schmitt (1993).

Previously, we identified four areas where males and females may differ in their reproductive behaviour, which can be traced back to these differing challenges that each sex has faced over an evolutionary timescale (Workman and Reader 2015):

- Asymmetry in potential number of offspring produced by each sex
- Duration of period of fertility
- Asymmetries in parental investment
- Cuckoldry.

Here we revisit and up-date these four areas.

ASYMMETRY IN POTENTIAL NUMBER OF OFFSPRING PRODUCED BY EACH SEX

Barring some rare exceptions, vertebrates reproduce sexually with males producing vast quantities of sperm and, in contrast, females producing a more limited number of eggs. In the case of humans, whereas a woman is limited to around 400 eggs (ova) which mature during her fertile years, during his fertile years a man can manufacture more than 10 million sperm every hour. Moreover, while the number of offspring a woman can produce is limited by the length of pregnancy (with inter-birth gaps), the number of offspring a man can produce is limited by the number of mating opportunities he has. In reality, of course, given female choice, and the fact that all human societies have developed moral codes concerning sexual behaviour, most males do not have unlimited mating opportunities. That said, we do see a much broader range of offspring production in men than in women. Men of high status in particular have a larger number of mating opportunities (Walter et al. 2020; Buss and Schmitt 2019). According to sexual strategies theory this helps to explain why men, cross-culturally, are more likely to seek status than women. It has also been used to explain high levels of competitiveness in male adolescents and relatively high levels of violence in this age group (Archer 2019).

DURATION OF PERIOD OF FERTILITY

One big difference between men and women is the age at which they cease to be fertile. Typically, a girl becomes fertile around the age of 13 and this fertility begins to drop off in women around the late thirties, terminating at menopause ('end of menstrual cycle') around 50. Boys also typically become fertile around 13, but, contrary to popular opinion, given there is no such thing as the 'male menopause', this can continue pretty much for the rest of a man's life. This means that, while human females are fertile for around 35 years, males can be fertile for 70 years or more. (Of course, men rarely impregnate women during their eighties or nineties but, astonishingly, this has been documented). The important point here is that ancestral males who chose younger women would most likely leave a larger number of surviving offspring than those who chose older women. In contrast there would not have been such strong selective pressures on ancestral women to choose young men. From this we can make two predictions. First, because fertility is more strongly correlated with youth in women than in men, men are more likely than women to have evolved to find signals of youthfulness physically attractive. Second, today, as men mature, they are more likely to marry (or at least attempt to court) women who are younger than themselves. A large amount of accumulated evidence appears to support both of these conjectures (Buss and Schmitt 2019).

ASYMMETRIES IN PARENTAL INVESTMENT

As discussed earlier, Trivers' theory of parental investment helped to solve Darwin's dilemma as to why males are the more competitive sex and females are more choosy when it comes to accepting 'suitors'. To recap, males compete for females because the latter invest highly in offspring production. That is, the minimum obligatory parental investment is substantially higher for females than for males. Females, for their part, are choosy about males as they want the latter either to invest in offspring or bring good genes into the equation. This asymmetry in parental investment means that males have less to lose if they make a poor choice, while females have a great deal to lose if they do. Despite this asymmetry in levels of investment, however, it pays both parties to make good decisions here. In the words of Buss and Schmitt:

> Good mate choices can bring a bounty of reproductive benefits, such as genes for healthy immune functioning, physical protection, and provisioning of resources for self and offspring. Poor mate choices can usher in a cascade of costs—sexually transmitted diseases ... a high mutation load, reputational damage, and abandonment.
>
> (Buss and Schmitt 2019, p. 79)

CUCKOLDRY

The term **cuckoldry** is derived from 'cuckoo', the bird which lays its eggs in other bird's nests. It refers to a man who, unknowingly, brings up another man's child (hence the similarity to the case of cuckoos). Since only men can be cuckolded (also known as **human non-paternity**), then those men who paid no attention to their female partner's behaviour with other men would be less likely to pass their genes on than those who paid closer attention. (Note that this is not a criticism specifically of female sexual conduct, as men must also have been 'misbehaving' in order for cuckoldry to take place!). Given that some studies suggest the rate of cuckoldry varies from around 1 per cent (Anderson 2006) to as high as 10 per cent (Baker and Bellis 1995; Voracek, Fisher and Shackelford 2009) we can predict that, cross-culturally, men are likely to develop anti-cuckoldry measures. Interestingly, evolutionists Martin Daly and Margo Wilson (1983) have related this to the fact that, cross-culturally, men attempt to control female behaviour. David Buss (2016) has conducted a number of studies which suggest men are more upset by infidelity than women (this is not to say women are impervious to sexual jealousy, see later).

In summary, due to these four areas where our male and female ancestors faced somewhat different adaptive challenges, we can anticipate some differences in current sexual strategies to have arisen in men and women. In fact, taking into account the four areas above, we can make quite specific predictions as to where these differences might lie. More specifically, given both a woman's limited number of ova and the limits to her length of fertility, we can

Figure 2.5 Common cuckoo being feed by distinctly smaller European robin

predict that men will have evolved preferences for youthfulness in partners. To evolutionary psychologists, youthfulness in women is a signal of high **reproductive value** (Williams 1975), a term that describes potential future offspring. Hence a girl of 17 has a much higher reproductive value than a woman of 37, for example. It does not, however, pay women to seek out youthfulness in a male since the latter are fertile for much longer and in fact more mature males are more likely to have gained wealth and status (see later). Taking into account differences in levels of parental investment, we can predict that women will look for signals of status, commitment and wealth in a man. We can also predict that men will be competitive (and on occasions aggressively so) towards other men over access to fertile women. Furthermore, given men are relatively high in parental investment (compared to other mammals), we can predict women will also be competitive for high status men. Finally, given they are the sex that can be cuckolded, we can predict that men will be more affected by a partner's sexual infidelity. In the remainder of this chapter we consider these predictions in greater detail. Considering all of these points together we can suggest that men and women will have evolved partially different mate choice criteria.

MATE CHOICE CRITERIA

Due to the work of David Buss and David Schmitt (alongside many others), evolutionists have now developed a much better understanding of the degree to which men and women differ (and how similar they are) when it comes to choosing a romantic partner. Some of these might be seen by some as 'common sense', but, the important point is that evolutionary psychologists have made use of sexual selection and parental investment theories to explain at an ultimate level what led to these differences. Here we consider a sub-set of such findings, that is, those derived directly from the four reasons why we can predict differences, as outlined above. These include age preferences/physical attractiveness, status and aggression, and cuckoldry and sexual jealousy. It should be noted that these are overlapping categories with, for example, aggression potentially being related to cuckoldry, mate retention and sexual jealousy.

BOX 2.3 IS THERE AN UNCONSCIOUS BIAS AGAINST MALES IN THE ACCEPTANCE OF SCIENTIFIC FINDINGS?

Here's a question for you. What is the term that describes dislike, hatred and distrust of women? You almost certainly know this to be **misogyny**. Here's another question which you might find more difficult. What is the term that describes dislike, hatred and distrust of men? In our experience, while nearly all students know the answer to the first question, hardly any are able to answer the second one. Why might this be the case? It would be ridiculous to suggest this does not exist. Might it be an example of unconscious bias against men? One recent research project examined the proposition that, due to ideologically based interpretations of scientific findings, people (both men and women) accept female-favouring findings of sex differences in abilities but reject male-favouring findings. Stewart-Williams, Chang, Wong, Jesse, Blackburn and Thomas (2021) presented participants (256 men and 236 women) with various versions of a fictional popular science article, which either demonstrated men or women were better at drawing (positive trait) or that lied more frequently (negative trait). They found that both sexes were more likely to trust the positive findings which favoured women. In particular, where findings were presented as favouring men, participants found them to less important, more offensive, harmful and upsetting than the reverse. (Note, these findings were largely duplicated in a similar study by Stewart-Williams, Wong, Chang and Thomas in 2022.) Stewart-Williams and co-workers suggest this unconscious bias against men is due to three factors. First, current stereotypes are more positive about women than men. Second, people perceive women as suffering more in society than men and want to redress this balance. And third, people (both women and men) are more protective of women – a situation that has been termed 'benevolent sexism' (Glick and Fiske 1997). Clearly, we should be objective when assessing scientific findings, as Stewart-Williams and colleagues point out, as misconceptions will ultimately harm relations between the sexes. Incidentally, for the record, the term that describes dislike, hatred and distrust of men is **misandry**.

AGE PREFERENCES AND PHYSICAL ATTRACTIVENESS

Clearly, reproductive value is not a concept that any man or woman considers when seeking out a romantic partner. Nevertheless, ancestral male hominins who sought out younger partners would most likely have passed on more copies of their genes, and in doing so would be passing on those genes involved in the development of that preference. This is because, so long as a female is sexually mature, signals of youth are likely to correlate with reproductive value. Hence, over an evolutionary timescale, signals of fertility will have come to be associated with standards of beauty in women (Toates, 2014). Physical signals that correlate both with fertility/reproductive value and with universal standards of beauty include, clear skin, suppleness, full lips, high cheekbones, small nose, symmetrical features, lustrous hair and a low waist-to-hip ratio (Symons 1979). Many studies across a large number of cultures verify the fact that men (and women) consider such features to be attractive female characteristics (Buss and Schmitt 2019). We should not, of course, imagine that physical appearance in men is of no importance to women. In fact, numerous studies have established that, while of less importance to women, there are physical features of men that are sought after. Cross-culturally, women prefer taller and more muscular men. Both of these, in turn, correspond to high status in men (Waynforth 2001; Geary, Vigil and Byrd-Craven 2004). In forager societies being tall and strong generally makes for better hunters and successful hunters in such groups have more romantic opportunities (Marlowe 2003). Having physical attributes that enhance hunting prowess is of little use in most countries today, but the preferences appear to remain, to the extent that currently taller men, for example, earn better salaries then shorter men (Stulp, Buunk and Pollet 2013) and have more mating opportunities and greater reproductive success (Pawlowki, Dunbar and Lipowicz 2000). Incidentally, of the last six American Presidents, all bar one have been over 6 foot (George W. Bush comes in a smidgen under 6 foot).

Returning to age, if men look for younger women this raises one important question. Is this conducive with the requirements of women? Do they prefer to have older men as their romantic partners? In fact, one of the earliest studies in the field of evolutionary psychology, that of David Buss, established back in 1989 that in every one of 37 cultures studied, women prefer older men and men prefer younger women (Buss 1989). This study, which had a sample of around 10,000, also helps to inform us of similarities (and differences) across cultures with regard to the other areas outlined above. This study is, of course, over 30 years old. It might be argued that social mores have changed since then and perhaps even our perception of romantic relationships. Some might suggest that, if replicated today, the findings would be quite different. Interestingly, an even larger scale study led be Kathryn Walter of the University of Santa Barbara was conducted in 2020. To the surprise of many, this sample of 14,000 spread across 45 countries uncovered almost identical findings. In particular, Walter et al. (2020) found that across cultures men were more interested in physical attractiveness and preferred younger women. On their side of the equation women continued show a significant preference for older men with good financial prospects. It appears that the effect is a robust one, both across time and place, suggesting these differences are the outcome of evolved preferences.

BOX 2.4 HOW DO WE KNOW THAT AN OBSERVED SEX DIFFERENCE IS EVOLUTIONARY IN ORIGIN?

Although most researchers accept that sex/gender differences exist in our species, there is much debate as to whether they are evolved features or whether they arose through social conditioning. In fact, many social scientists are critical of evolutionary explanations, suggesting instead that any differences between the sexes are largely or entirely due to the way society treats men and women differently right from birth (Bussey and Bandura 1999; Hyde 2014). It is certainly the case that social influences affect the roles that males and females come to adopt. But evolutionary psychologists would suggest that such learning is influenced by our evolutionary history and (most) boys and girls tend to gravitate towards 'gender appropriate' roles. The question remains, what sort of evidence suggests there is an evolutionary contribution in the development of these differences. Based on the work of previous evolutionists, evolutionary social psychologist John Archer (2019) has developed a list of six criteria that can be taken as evidence that sex differences are evolutionary in origin. We paraphrase these as six questions below:

1 Is there a credible, adaptive explanation that can be tested?
2 Do we observe a similar difference in other species (especially in primates)?
3 Is the observed difference found across cultures (especially in forager people)?
4 Does this difference occur early in life or at puberty? Is it pronounced in young adults?
5 Is this difference associated with differences in sex hormones?
6 Are adaptive design features seen in mechanisms underlying the sex difference?

Note that for a sex difference to be considered evolutionary in origin, it does not have to fulfil every single one of the above. The more of these it does fulfil, however, the stronger the argument that such a difference is related to sexual selection.

STATUS AND AGGRESSION

Across human societies, males strive for and signal status and dominance (Barkow 1989). While much of this is achieved through impressing or intimidating other males, when they observe serious competition, men are far more likely than women to respond with physical aggression (Archer 2019). Why should this be the case? Given that physical contests peak for men during their peak fertility years (late-teenage and early adulthood) and, given that comparable male–male aggressive interactions also occur in other mammals when competing for females, it seems likely that this is a sexually selected adaptation (or at least it would have been during our evolutionary history). Hence, we can see this increase in physical aggression which potentially increases within-group status as having arisen via intrasexual selection. Interestingly, there is a link between circulating testosterone and dominance in males at this stage in life, which adds strength to the notion that aggression and dominance are related to an evolutionary history of inter-male competition (Archer 2019). Moreover, inter-male physical aggression is typically more prolonged and more intense than is inter-female physical aggression. This sex difference is true not only for humans but also for primate species in general, adding weight to the argument that this sex difference arose through sexual selection (Archer 2019). In relation to status, as Buss (2016) has pointed out, 'along with status come better food, more abundant territory, and superior health care'. The evidence that status leads both to greater sexual opportunities and to greater inclusive fitness is overwhelming. One study of 186 societies ranging from the Aleut of Alaska to the Mbuti of Africa showed that men of high status have significantly more wives, greater wealth and better nourished children than those lower down the pecking order (Betzig 1986).

CUCKOLDRY AND SEXUAL JEALOUSY

As we have seen, because only men can be cuckolded, it is predicted that they are more likely to be susceptible to suspicions that

Figure 2.6 Sexually mature male gelada baboon aggressively displaying in Debre Libanos, Ethiopia

their partners have had a sexual relationship with another man. This does not, of course, suggest that women are not affected by jealousy. If a man forms an attachment to another woman, then they might lose support and resources. Because of these differences Buss and Schmitt's sexual strategies theory leads to the prediction that intense jealousy will be evoked by subtly different circumstances in men and women. It is predicted that men will be more affected by the possibility of their partner having sex with another and women are more affected by thoughts that their partner has fallen in love with another. The question is how might we possibly test such a hypothesis? In fact, over the last 30 years researchers have developed a multitude of methods in order to answer this question. These include self-reports following actual infidelities, lab-experiments of physiological responses while imaging various forms of infidelity and neuro-imaging studies. Buss and Schmitt (2019) maintain that all of these support the notion that men are more affected by sexual infidelity than by emotional infidelity and the reverse being the case for women. An example of this is the fact that, when participants imagined their partners either falling in love or having sexual intercourse with a rival, clear sex differences emerged. In fact, in comparison with women, men showed a much greater increase in heart rate and higher levels of electrodermal activity when imagining the sexual scenario. Women, in contrast, showed significantly higher responses to emotional infidelity (Buss et al. 1992). In his review of the area, however, Archer (2019) suggested that findings of sex differences in this area, while significant, are not always large.

SHORT-TERM RELATIONSHIPS

The examples above show clear, if not always large, differences in the features that men and women favour when considering a romantic partner. They also demonstrate differences in behaviour such as levels of physical aggression or the circumstances that provide the greatest degree of negative response. Because we are concerned with how the process of sexual selection can drive the sexes apart, it is appropriate that we focus on these differences. It would be remiss of us, however, not to point out that there are many areas where men and women show very similar responses even when it comes to matters of the heart. Buss's original 1989 study found that both men and women place emotional closeness and commitment as their most important feature in a partner. In fact, the differences in importance of physical attraction and status are both secondary to these features. Put simply, for long-term relationships, in all cultures both sexes seek romantic love from a partner. You may have noticed we prefaced that last statement with the phrase 'for long-term relationships'; because the requirements of men and women dovetail nicely when forming an enduring pair bond (producing and raising children), this is perhaps not surprising. When it comes to one-off relationships, however, things turn out to be really quite different.

Although the acceptability of short-term relationships (including 'one-night stands') varies greatly between societies, all cultures studied have been found to engage in such assignations (Buss 2016). This raises the question – why? From an evolutionary perspective, it may pay both sexes to gain variety in their offspring (recalling from Chapter 1 that the very existence of sex as a form of reproduction may be due to the increase in variability that it leads to). In addition to the increase in variety in offspring that short-term relationships lead to, there may also be differences from an ultimate perspective between men and women in why they engage is such behaviour.

SHORT-TERM RELATIONSHIPS WHAT'S IN IT FOR WOMEN?

As we saw earlier, while men are limited in their reproductive output by their access to women, women are unlikely to increase their reproductive output by sleeping with more than one man. Also, we have to bear in mind that, if women make poor choices, then the costs are always higher for them than for men under similar circumstances. Putting all of this together, it has long been a scientific conundrum as to why women engage in short-term relationships at all? What possible selective advantage might women have from activity such as 'hook-ups' and one-night stands? Buss and Schmitt (1993) think they may have the answer. In fact, they consider they have identified four possible selective advantages for women in having short-term relationships:

- Immediate resources
- Good genes
- Evaluating short-term mates for possible long-term relationships
- Mate switching.

In terms of immediate resources, ancestral women living under desperate conditions, such as during a hard winter, might have gained life-saving food and shelter from forming a relatively brief sexual relationship with a man. It is certainly the case that in a number of forager societies this form of strategy is utilized in times of hardship (Buss 2019; Symons 1979). In the case of good genes, it is well established that women who have affairs tend to do so with men who have more attractive masculine features (a signal of potential good genes) than their current partner (Buss and Schmitt 2019). In relation to making use of a short-term relationship to evaluate a potential long-term partner, it is known that women regularly report falling in love with a man they had originally anticipated having a 'fling' with (Buss 2016). This evidence can also be applied to the mate switching hypothesis as 79% of women questioned about extra-marital relationships report falling in love with men they had an affair with (Buss, 2016).

SHORT-TERM RELATIONSHIPS WHAT'S IN IT FOR MEN?

Since men are potentially able to increase their reproductive output/inclusive fitness through increasing the number of mating opportunities, we are not faced with the same sort of adaptive conundrum we saw when considering women. The notion that men are distinctly less coy than women about engaging in a sexual relationship may seem a blindingly obvious statement to those living in industrialised nations. For this to work as an evolutionary explanation, however, it is necessary that this pattern is observed cross-culturally. While patterns of premarital sex have been observed to vary greatly across cultures, in all cultures studied men have been found to exhibit four patterns of behaviour that support the notion of an adaptive response to increase inclusive fitness (Buss and Schmitt 1993; 2019):

- Men express greater desire for short-term relationships than women
- Men desire a larger number of sexual partners than women

- Men are willing to engage in sex after a shorter period than women
- Men relax their 'standards' for short-term mating opportunities compared to women.

In conclusion, there are differences between the sexes in their mate choice criteria when considering long-term pair bonds. These include a greater emphasis on physical attractiveness for men and a greater emphasis on status and resources for women. Despite this, for such relationships, men and women show distinct similarities. Both place a premium on emotional closeness, good nature and being dependable over and above physical attractiveness or status. It is when we consider short-term 'hook-ups' that we can most easily tease the sexes apart. Women increase their criteria – men decrease theirs.

BOX 2.5 THE SUPERIOR SEX: DO WOMEN ULTIMATELY HAVE THE LAST LAUGH?

You might at this point wonder whether evolution has provided men with a number of advantages over women. You may even be forgiven for thinking that two male authors take pleasure in repeatedly pointing out that the dice appear to be loaded in favour of men. Males, for example, have a much lower obligate parental investment and they are able to form relationships with younger women (although they are of course the only sex which can be cuckolded). To redress this balance, it is worth pointing out that recent scientific findings suggest that women are in many ways the genetically superior sex. A recent book by Sharon Moalem sets out a series of home truths:

> Women have stronger immune systems. Women are less likely to suffer from developmental disability, are more likely to see the world in a variety of colours, and overall are better at fighting cancer. Women are simply stronger than men at every stage of life.
>
> (Moalem 2020, p.1)

To top it all, women live an average of seven years longer than men. It would be beyond the scope of this book to examine all of the genetic reasons for these advantages, but, in a nutshell, this is largely down to the fact that women have two X chromosomes whereas men have one X and one Y. While the much smaller Y chromosome is required for the production of testosterone in young adulthood, it also suppresses the immune system later in life. Also, the extra X chromosome provides a degree of protection in women. It is humbling for men to realise that, in the game of life, ultimately we are the weaker sex.

SUMMARY

In *The Descent of Man* Darwin developed the second selective force – sexual selection where the opposite sex acts as the selector rather than the forces of nature. Intrasexual selection consists of competition between members of one sex for access to the opposites sex and intersexual selection is concerned with impressing the opposite sex. Sexual reproduction appears to have evolved in order to increase variability in offspring. One prominent theory suggests this variability is of particular importance in providing various forms of resistance to potential invading pathogens. Robert Trivers developed parental investment theory, which proposes the sex which invests most highly in offspring (usually female) will be maximally choosy, whereas the other sex (usually male) will be maximally competitive for access to the highly investing sex. Sexual selection and parental investment have become important theories to help explain the origin of sex differences in behaviour – including humans. While the concept of competitive males was well accepted in Darwin's day, the notion of female choice was not. Today female choice has become a well-accepted phenomenon helping to drive the males of a species towards adaptations that are designed to impress females. Female choice can help us to understand why males are often more elaborately coloured and more likely to be risk-takers. Sexual strategies theory, which has been developed by David Buss and David Schmitt, suggests current sex differences in mate choice criteria and in other aspects of psychological make-up can be traced back to different challenges faced by men and women in the ancestral past. We suggest differences between the sexes can be traced back to: the potential number of offspring produced by each sex, the duration of fertility, asymmetries in parental investment and the possibility of cuckoldry. Over the last 30 years, evidence has accumulated that important features males rate highly include youth and physical attractiveness whereas females prefer somewhat older partners of status. Both sexes, however, rate emotional maturity and commitment as more important than the above characteristics, at least in a long-term partner. This means that for long-term pair-bonded relationships men and women are really quite similar. For short-term relationships, however, men reduce their standards whereas women increase theirs.

FURTHER READING

Buss, D. M. (2016) *The Evolution of Desire: Strategies of Human Mating*. New York: Basic Books.

Toates, F. (2014) *How Sexual Desire Works: The Enigmatic Urge*. Cambridge: Cambridge University Press.

Zuc, M. and Simmons, L. W. (2018) *Sexual Selection: A Very Brief Introduction*. Oxford: Oxford University Press.

3

LIVING WITH OTHERS

EVOLUTION, SOCIAL BEHAVIOUR AND MORALITY

Outside of the social insects (bees, wasps, ants and termites) and curios such as naked mole rats (see Box 3.1) *Homo sapiens* is probably the most social species of animal on the planet. And a very successful one. If we were to gather together all of the mammals on earth and put them on a suitably large set of weighing scales, it is estimated that humans would account for 34 per cent of the total weight. Perhaps even more astonishingly 61 per cent is our livestock (principally cattle). Of the remaining 5 per cent, 1 per cent is accounted for by our pets with only 4 per cent being wild mammals such as elephants and rats. In many respects we have turned the planet into a gigantic factory designed to sustain our massive numbers. The reasons for this population explosion are various – a reduction in child mortality, improved healthcare and sanitation, intensive agricultural practices, but underlying all of these factors is our ability to cooperate with one another and, as we shall see, cooperation has a dark side.

Social psychologists have made great progress in understanding how our species interact with one another, exploring important topics such as cooperation, inter-group conflict and stereotyping. What they have not done, because it is not part of mainstream social psychology, is to ask the ultimate questions: what are the **fitness** benefits to individuals and their genes of cooperating, why do groups get into conflict, what is the evolutionary function (if any) of stereotyping? We don't promise to answer all of these questions, but we discuss some of them.

DOI: 10.4324/9780429274428-3

Underpinning many aspects of social behaviour is morality. We often judge harshly those who refuse to cooperate and glorify altruists, vilify members of other groups and praise our own. Later in this chapter we discuss what morality might be for and how it relates to social behaviour in general and cooperation in particular.

COOPERATION AMONG KIN

Superficially, cooperation seems to pose a problem for evolution as many believe that evolution promotes selfishness, but actually the opposite is true. Consider our sex organs. At the ultimate level these are not for you at all, rather they are ways in which genes can escape one body where they can blend with the genes of another body and, after a sufficient period of time escape into the outside world in the form of a brand new person. How does it survive? Well, the genes have already thought of that by engineering structures on the female body that enable their new host to survive and thrive. They have also engineered the minds of the two parents to fall in love with it and care for it until it can live an independent life.

To see how this works, imagine that at some distant point in history there was an ancestor of ours that didn't offer much in the way of childcare. As you might imagine, although some of their offspring might have survived to reproductive age, many of them would not. Now imagine that a gene (or some combination of genes) arrived through mutation that made the parents fall in love with their child and invest heavily in them. Such childcare was certainly more costly to the parents in terms of time, effort and resources but the benefits to their offspring in terms of the likelihood that they survived to reproductive was much larger than the cost to the parents.

Of course, these offspring would very likely inherit these childcare genes from their parents so that when they grew up and had their own children they would care for them in the same way that their parents did. You can imagine that the enhanced survival rate of such children would lead to the gene increasing in frequency over the generations until it became the norm.

This is the logic that underlies Hamilton's rule (Hamilton 1964), which we met in Chapter 1, so long as the benefit to the child (B) is greater than the cost to the parent (C) divided by the likelihood that the gene that is in the parent, is also in the child (r).

The equation is below and has been rearranged to reflect this way of thinking (the equation means exactly the same as in its more standard form): $B > C/r$. The bigger the value of r the bigger the cost the parent can bear. And this equation does not just apply to parents, it applies to any form of genetic relatedness. To recap what we discussed in Chapter 1, passing on genes by having babies is called direct fitness but you can also pass on genes another way. A full sibling shares 50 per cent of genes with you (just like offspring) if she has a child then the likelihood that that child would share a particular gene is 25 per cent. This is because that child's genes have undergone a further 'dilution' as a result of it having half your sister's genes and half from the child's father. Your relatedness to the child, let's say it is your niece, (r) is 25 per cent. So you will bear approximately half of the cost for a niece as you would for your own child but you would still help out. Passing genes on in this way is known as indirect fitness. Direct fitness and indirect fitness are together referred to as **inclusive fitness**. To add another technical word we call the tendency to favour kin 'nepotism', so organisms that act to favour kin are called **nepotistic strategists**.

BOX 3.1 KIN SELECTION IN NAKED MOLE RATS AND HUMAN EVOLUTION

There are many examples of cooperative mammals other than humans. Meerkats for one whose cuteness has led them to become so effective at selling insurance. Sadly, this is an occupation that is unlikely to be bestowed upon the naked mole rat (see Figure 3.1, if you dare). Looking a bit like a deflated balloon with teeth, the naked mole rat lives in underground communities across Africa. Apart from their looks, what makes them special is that their lifestyle is much more like that of the eusocial insects rather than mammals. Each colony has only one breeding female, the queen. The non-breeding members of the colony engage in tasks such as digging the tunnels that they live in, childcare and defending the colony. It used to be thought that naked mole rats engage in their highly

Figure 3.1 A naked mole rat

cooperative behaviour as a result of inbreeding which cranked up their coefficient of relatedness so that they would bear an even greater cost for the benefit of other members. But more recent research suggests this is not the case (Ingram et al. 2015). Naked mole rats are not particularly in-bred, their genetic relatedness is similar to those of their siblings. So what leads to their cooperative behaviour? So far the best explanation is that their reproductive system is more akin to something called **cooperative breeding** in which relatives help out in child care and other duties (Szafranski et al. 2022). Somewhat surprisingly, recent research has suggested that our hunter–gatherer ancestors may also have engaged in cooperative breeding. Sarah Hrdy (2017) presents evidence that hunter–gatherer parents could not have provided enough calories for the families partly due to the long period of infant-dependence which made gathering food difficult for mothers.

So other family members (principally grandparents and older siblings) stepped in, and even in some cases unrelated people who didn't have families themselves. So maybe the origins of our sociality lies in the helplessness of our offspring.

We can see that naked mole rats are nepotistic strategists generally adhering to Hamilton's rule, but what about our species?

BLOOD IS THICKER THAN WATER

Imagine that a runaway train is steaming towards a group of your friends and relatives, who, unaccountably, are standing on the tracks. You have time to save just one. Who would you choose? When Eugene Burnstein and his colleagues presented this scenario to a group of young adults, they found the results fitted Hamilton's prediction that participants helping behaviour was strongly related to degree of relatedness (Burnstein, Crandall and Kitayama 1994, see Figure 3.2). Here, degree of relatedness is expressed as a proportion (out of one) rather than a percentage. Similar findings were presented in research by Masden et al. (2007) who asked participants to perform ski-squats (an increasingly painful exercise where one squats with ones back against a wall as if sitting on a chair, but without the chair). Participants were either from London or rural southern Africa and were told that the longer they could do this the more reward would be given to individuals of different relatedness. As before participants squatted for longer when rewarding those closest to them. There was no difference between the different groups of participants.

Another way of testing Hamilton's theory of kin selection has been to consider historical accounts of behaviour towards kin. One such study considered the role of **kin altruism** in Viking invaders in Iceland and Scotland. Evolutionist Robin Dunbar in collaboration with Amanda Clark and Nicola Hurst found that, between

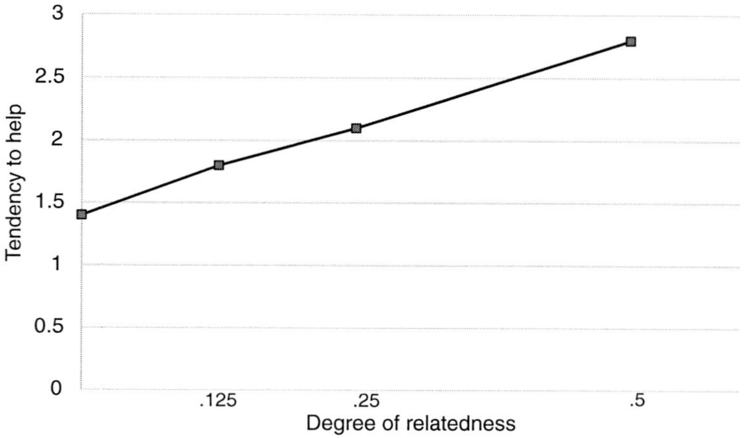

Figure 3.2 The tendency to help as a function of the degree of relatedness of the person. (Redrawn by authors)

the tenth and twentieth century, Viking alliances that were formed between kin were significantly more stable than those between non-kin (Dunbar, Clark and Hurst 1995). Moreover, kinship reduced the likelihood of committing murder to gain resources except when the potential benefits were very high.

COOPERATING WITH NON-RELATIVES

In 1958 the economist Leonard Read published a book called *I, Pencil*. The book was written from the perspective of a pencil who claimed that 'not a single person on the face of this earth knows how to make me'. Sounds crazy? Well, if you think about it, it really isn't. The kind of pencil being described is your basic wooden pencil, but someone has to get that wood. Getting that wood requires someone to have created for you, say, an axe to chop down the tree. Making that axe requires someone of have fashioned the steel head, the steel needed to have been turned into iron, the iron dug out of the ground. And of course, while all of these people are busy making these objects someone needs to grow, process and prepare food for them. Then we need to consider the paint on the pencil, the graphite, the little bit of rubber at the top. All put together, the pencil is correct in its assertion that 'no one' person knows how to make me. This level of cooperation cannot be explained by Hamilton's rule, since in order for it to work, r – the coefficient of relatedness – needs to be above zero and, quite bluntly, no one has that many close relatives. And that is just for a humble wooden pencil topped by an eraser. How big would a family need to be to make a mobile phone, a car, an aircraft? Most certainly enough to make a family get together somewhat difficult.

Happily, there are theories that enable cooperation to exist between non-relatives, and the most famous and most discussed of these is that provided by the biologist Robert Trivers.

Trivers has made a vast contribution to evolutionary theory, introducing and refining concepts such as parental investment theory (see Chapter 2), parent–offspring conflict and a theory of self-deception, but is perhaps best known for his theory of **reciprocal altruism** which was first published in 1971. The logic of reciprocal altruism is familiar to all of us. If I have some food and you do not then I can share my food with you, but of course, although this benefits you it is costly to me which would put me at a competitive disadvantage. However, if later on I have no food and, remembering my favour, you give some food to me, then the costs and benefits even out. This may sound trivial, like exchanging birthday cards, but in an ancestral environment where food may be scarce, such exchanges could be a matter of life or death. And exchanges do not need to be like-for-like. Someone might share food in return for another helping them build a shelter or defending them from a predator or rival. In the time that has passed since Trivers first proposed this idea, most evolutionists have dropped the 'altruism', instead referring to it as 'reciprocation'. This is because if a favour or resource is given with the expectation of the recipient reciprocating at a later date it cannot be called truly altruistic.

There is an obvious problem with reciprocity. If I were to share food with you but you failed to reciprocate when I was in a position of need then that would obviously place me at a competitive disadvantage to you. This is known as the **free rider** problem as the non-reciprocator is taking a 'free ride': taking the benefit without paying the price. Therefore, in order for this system to work effectively there need to be some conditions placed on such exchanges.

- The benefit of the act should usually be greater for the recipient than the cost is to the actor.
- Organisms engaging in such exchanges should be able to recognise and remember past interactions and their outcomes (to discriminate between cooperators and free riders).
- Organisms should be sufficiently long-lived so that they can repeatedly enter exchanges with the same cooperating individuals.

To the above we might also add that there should be some way of dealing with free riders, either by refusing to cooperate with them if they have defaulted in the past, or by punishing them in some way. As we shall see in Chapter 5, Cosmides and Tooby (1992) have found evidence that humans are rather good at identifying those who have taken the benefit without paying the price.

There is some evidence that such reciprocation occurs in non-humans. One of the most famous examples is the exchange of blood in vampire bats (Wilkinson 1984) and there is also some evidence in non-human primates, but otherwise most examples of non-human cooperation is limited (Clutton-Brock 2009) or can be explained by means other than reciprocity. For humans, however, it is a very different matter with a wealth of evidence from anthropological observations relating to food sharing (e.g. Ziker and Schnegg 2005) and experiments in which participants play various cooperation games (Andreoni and Miller 1993). Not all of these studies paint a happy picture of reciprocation as it seems that there is often a temptation for people to either take a little more than is due to them or to give a little less back than is required. For example, in so-called public good games, participants are given a sum of money (say £10) and can anonymously contribute some, all or none of it to a central pot. The experimenter then multiplies this by a certain amount (say they double it) and then divides this amount equally among the participants. So, if there are ten participants and each puts in the full £10 so that the pot contains £100, this would be doubled and each person would receive £20. You can imagine that if things continued in this way for long enough everyone would make quite a lot of money. If they all invest the £20 then everyone gets £40, then £80 and so on. Sadly, this is not what typically happens. Someone usually realises that he or she can buck the system by putting in a little less, or even nothing. To see how this would work imagine that everyone puts in their initial £10 apart from our cheat who puts in nothing to give a grand total of £90, this is doubled and divided among all ten participants who all receive £18 but of course our dirty cheat put nothing in the pot and so he or she has the £18 plus the initial stake to give a total of £28. Of course, the others aren't stupid and quickly realise by the fact that they are getting less than they should that someone is putting in less than their full share, and respond by under contributing themselves with the end result that cooperation collapses and no one makes anything (Fehr and Schmidt 1999).

There are solutions to this problem, for example if members are able to levy fines or other punishments against those who under contribute to bring them into line (Fehr and Gächter 2000). But it must also be pointed out that most instances of reciprocity are not between random, anonymous strangers but between friends, acquaintances and colleagues – people who know each other, or at least know *of* each other – and people are much less likely to default on people they know and who know them (Nowak, 2006). Important as well is one's reputation. If one has a reputation as a cheat, it is unlikely that anyone would trust you enough for you to be able to exploit that trust (Nowak and Sigmund, 2005). Nowak's work adds a somewhat different type of reciprocity, **indirect reciprocity**. In indirect reciprocity having a reputation as a reciprocator will lead people to share with you, even if you haven't previously shared with them in the belief that you will. So maintaining a good reputation can be an important motivator against cheating. Of course, it is sometimes possible to fake a good reputation to exploit others – something that happens frequently on the internet, which is why there are websites such as Trustpilot, TrustedSite, ScamAdvisor in order to help us tell the cheats from the champions.

BOX 3.2 THE CINDERELLA EFFECT

Evolutionists Martin Daly and Margo Wilson spent more than 40 years examining family conflict from an evolutionary perspective. One of their most shocking findings is that when a family contains a stepfather the chances of a child being physically harmed are greatly increased, with, for example, the rate of recorded infanticide being 120 times higher for stepfathers than for biological fathers (Daly and Wilson, 1998). Of course, such abuse and infanticide is rare in such families, it is just more common than in families without a stepfather. Daly and Wilson call this the Cinderella effect (Daly and Wilson, 1998) after the fairy story where a stepchild is mistreated by the rest of the family and use kin selection to explain this difference in levels of abuse, suggesting that because stepchildren are not genetically related to their stepparents they may not always release the kind of caring behaviour that we normally expect from biological parents. As you might expect the Cinderella effect has been disputed (e.g. Buller, 2005), but Daly and Wilson have produced well developed, data-driven rebuttals to such criticisms (Daly and Wilson, 2005; 2007).

IN-GROUP, OUT-GROUP BIAS AND CONFLICT: THE DARKER SIDE OF SOCIALITY

In 1971 a team of psychologists conducted a study that has had far-reaching consequences and tells us much about our nature as a species. The team was led by Henri Tajfel who was born in Poland in 1919 and was Jewish. Following the outbreak of the Second World War he was imprisoned in a series of concentration camps. When he finally returned home, he realised that he was one of the lucky ones: few of his close friends and none of his close family had survived. Later Tajfel moved to Britain where he studied psychology, eventually becoming a successful researcher and professor. According to Mick Billig, one of his research students, the question that most preoccupied Tajfel was, perhaps unsurprisingly, 'How is genocide possible?' (Billig, 2002).

At the time it was thought that in order for a group to act negatively towards another group there needed to be a lot below the surface. Maybe a common language, or a long cultural history. Maybe there needed to be ideological or religious conflict between the two groups, flags, banners and national anthems? Tajfel's deceptively simple idea was to strip away all of these things and see if people could be made to act prejudicially towards the out-group and favour the in-group in a matter of seconds. He called this the 'minimal group paradigm'.

In one of a sequence of studies a group of teenage boys were presented individually (it was important that none of the participants ever met each other in the lab) with a series of paintings by Paul Klee and Wassily Kandinsky (for representative examples see Figure 3.3) They were not told which artworks were by which painter, were not familiar with the paintings which were labelled as either A or B. They were then asked whether they preferred the work of painter A or B, not being told who A and B were. They were then randomly assigned to a condition of being a liker of Klee or liker of B (Tajfel, Billig, Bundy and Flamant, 1971).

Later, each participant was approached and told that they had been specially selected to allocate payment to the other participants; they themselves would receive no reward. They were given slips of paper containing numbers that represented the reward to be

Figure 3.3 (a) Paintings by Paul Klee (left); (b) Wassily Kandinsky (right) as used in the study by Tajfel (1970)

given to the fans of Klee or Kandinsky. These rewards fell into three different allocation patterns.

1 Maximum joint profit (which gave both in- and out-group the largest amount)
2 Maximum in-group profit (which had the largest amount for the in-group)
3 Maximum difference (which maximised the difference between the in- and out-groups in the in-group's favour but with a smaller amount to the in-group overall than either 1 or 2).

If participants were egalitarian and simply wanted everyone to get the largest reward irrespective of their 'group' they would choose 1, if they were interested in simply getting the most for their own 'group' they would choose 2. But bizarrely they didn't; the majority of participants chose to maximise the difference between the two 'groups' even if that meant getting less for their own 'group' in absolute terms.

What this study shows (and there have been many replications and modifications over the years) is two things. First of all, groups can be created on the flimsiest of evidence (that is why we have been putting inverted commas round the word group). These aren't groups in any real sense with history, rituals, affiliation and meaning; they are random aggregations of individuals unified only by a meaningless label. The second thing is that even on the basis of next to nothing at all you can create prejudice of a kind. It is not enough for the in-group to do well; they must also do better than the out-group.

You might argue that this experiment is somewhat artificial, and you would be 100 per cent correct. And that is the point. If in-group favouritism and out-group prejudice can be created so swiftly and on such scant foundation, think of what might happen when the group *does* have solemn rituals, colourful flags and an uplifting national anthem?

But what, if anything, does this mean in evolutionary terms? One answer is that it is evidence that our evolutionary history was one of inter-group conflict with neighbouring tribes fighting over resources and territory (Keeley, 1996). In order to better protect ourselves against invading outsiders we evolved a sense of group-mindedness that would permit group cohesion and a sense of 'all for one and one for all'. Your group identity would generally only become salient when there was a potential for conflict with an out-group, and it is this tendency the Tajfel study was triggering, although in this case the conflict was mild, simply the allocation of rewards.

This is largely similar to our previous discussions of cooperation, although here our cooperative tendencies are biased towards members of our group, what is sometimes called **parochial altruism**. Using computer simulations, Choi and Bowles found that in situations of conflict, groups containing parochial altruists were more successful than groups whose members did not favour the in-group, suggesting that being biased towards the in-group is effective in conflict situations. In experiments conducted on indigenous groups in Papua New Guinea, Bernhard, Fischbacher and Fear (2006) found that participants were much more likely to protect members of the in-group than that of the out-group (see also, Reader and Hughes 2020).

There is also some evidence that, particularly during times of conflict, there is an emphasis on encouraging members of the in-group to cooperate to further increase group cohesion. For example, Rebers and Koopmans (2012) found that in games similar to the public goods game described above, participants were much more likely to punish members for under contributing when their group was in competition with an out group. Furthermore, Price, Cosmides and Tooby (2002) found that when participants were given a scenario whereby they were asked whether they would participate in a war against a hostile country, those who agreed to participate were prepared to sanction punishments to those who refused to participate.

We have merely scratched the surface in our discussions of evolutionary social psychology, and there is still much work to do. The picture that is emerging is of a species that is born to cooperate. In the next section we will look at the role that morality plays in this cooperative process.

MORALITY

When we think of morality, it is often big issues that spring to mind. Is it morally correct to turn off a life support system when the patient has little chance of regaining consciousness? Is assisted dying wrong? Does contributing to food banks just encourage employers to continue paying their staff poorly? Important though these questions are, morality is important in regulating many of the smaller aspects of life as well. Is it justified to jump a queue when you are in a rush? Is it OK for someone to sit in a stationary car with the engine running? When someone asks you whether you like their new dress, should you be honest? When we consider morality from an evolutionary perspective, it is important to think of morality in a broader sense then we are perhaps used to doing because we make moral decisions all the time.

RELATIONAL MODELS THEORY

The anthropologist Alan Fiske and his colleague Tage Shakti Rai argue that morality exists for the express purpose of managing our social relationships effectively. Fiske's **relational models theory** proposes there are four fundamental relationships; here we discuss just the three that we consider to be evolutionarily fundamental. These relationships relate to community, reciprocity and hierarchy.

Community relationships (what Fiske calls **community sharing**) involve obligations towards your group (perhaps best thought of as an ancestral tribe) which permits group-minded cohesion that enables their group to function properly and compete with rival groups. Fiske calls the morals of community sharing **unity** and these relate to respecting the history and traditions of the group, the identification of individuals with the fate of the group and rules governing the equal sharing of food and other resources (Bowles and Gintis, 2000). The morals of community sharing can be summed up by the phrase 'all for one and one for all' including care for those who are sick or injured and a feeling of collective responsibility (even shame) if a community member transgresses the community's rules. It is noteworthy that under these morals, care and resources are freely shared without the expectation that the favours are returned. In fact, direct reciprocation under community sharing would be inappropriate: Fiske gives the example of inviting your friends round for dinner and then asking for payment.

Reciprocal relationships (what Fiske calls **equality matching**) exist between equal parties. This is very close to Trivers' notion of reciprocal altruism. In such a relationship individuals agree to work together and share the work out equally. Fiske calls these morals those of **equality**. Or one person may offer a favour to another. Unlike the community sharing relationship, however, there is an expectation that the recipient reciprocates at some later point. Reciprocation could either be like-for-like (both help the other to build a house, for example) or maybe 'in kind' person A helps person B build a house and person B reciprocates by giving a spear to person A. The morals of equality matching are straightforward: pay what you are due to pay, or suffer the consequences. (Fiske provides a fourth kind of relationship, **market pricing**, which is similar to equality matching but involves the exchange of tokens such as money. We do not describe this further as it is an extension of equality matching and not evolutionarily basic or distinct.)

The final relationship type are hierarchical relationships (Fiske calls this **authority ranking** and the associated morals that govern it **hierarchy**) and these involve some individuals – parents, tribal elders, leaders, gods – having a higher status and thereby commanding respect and obedience from those lower down in the pecking order. Subordinates are expected to obey and respect superiors – whether they be parents, leaders or gods – and to punish those who defile or show disrespect to superiors. For their part, superiors are expected to guide, nurture and protect those who are subordinate to them. Unlike community sharing and equality matching where everyone is equal, the morals of hierarchy are asymmetrical. Those lower in the hierarchy are expected to show respect to and follow the commands of those higher up.

By following the morals relevant to each of these categories we ensure that the different kinds of relationships are successfully managed and that individuals within these groups cooperate to the benefit of everyone within the group.

It is important to point out, however, that Fiske's version of morality isn't always sweetness and light. Fiske argues that violence of various kinds is frequently used to ensure that people conform to societal rules and lists honour killings, the death penalty and genocide as natural consequences of morality. Honour killings because a person has contravened the rules of community; the death penalty for murder as a result of the eye-for-an-eye logic of equality matching; and genocide as a result of people placed so low in the hierarchy they are judged to be subhuman. And, of course, the perpetrators were only 'following orders' from those higher up. Fiske and Rai call this **virtuous violence**. Virtuous violence sounds contradictory: how can violence possibly be virtuous? What Fiske means here is that people often do things that we might consider to be bad, but do so for what they consider to be good reasons. As Fiske and Rai say in their book:

> Except for a few psychopaths, hardly anybody harming anybody else is doing something that they intend to be evil. On the contrary, they intend to be doing something right and good.
>
> (Fiske and Rai, 2014)

In support of this point Fiske and Rai list examples such as genocide, female genital mutilation and honour killings as atrocities whereby the perpetrator believes that they are in the right.

MORALITY AS COOPERATION (MAC)

Evolutionary psychologist Oliver Curry, like Fiske, proposes that morality is a solution to managing cooperation within groups (making this explicit in calling his theory Morality As Cooperation or MAC for short). Whereas Fiske collected cross-cultural evidence and looked for common features across societies, Curry's starting point was to investigate the ecological problems that confront humans living in groups (see Table 3.1). There are some similarities with Fiske's scheme as both place an emphasis on reciprocal exchange and community relations, but MAC separates out kin relationships and group loyalty as we did in Chapter 1. Curry further divides Fiske's authority ranking into heroism (dominance) and deference and adds fairness where resources are shared equally or according to need and special morals concerned with ownership of resources of land.

Curry, Mullins and Whitehouse (2019) compared their moral scheme against the stated morals from 60 different countries from all continents (bar Antarctica) and found that there was a high level of agreement between these and the morals specified in MAC.

There are many other attempts to understand morality but so far the approaches put forward by Fiske and Rai and Curry seem the

Table 3.1 Oliver Curry's 'periodic table of morality'

Domain	*Virtues*	*Vices*
Family	Duty of care, special obligations to kin	Incest, neglect
Group	Loyalty, unity, solidarity, conformity	Betrayal, treason
Reciprocity	Reciprocity, trustworthiness, forgiveness.	Cheating, ingratitude
Heroism	Bravery, fortitude, largesse	Cowardice, miserliness
Deference	Respect, obedience, humility	Disrespect, hubris
Fairness	Fairness, impartiality, equality	Unfairness, favouritism
Property	Respect for property, property rights	Theft, trespass

Source: adapted from Curry (2016).

most plausible, as both have at their heart the need to manage relationships with significant others.

SUMMARY

Humans are pre-eminently social beings and it is partly our ability to cooperate with one another that has led to such a position of dominance on our planet, for good or for bad. One way that we can explain cooperation is through kin selection whereby genes can evolve that enable us to help close relatives. This is common in both human and non-human species. Humans also frequently cooperate with non-kin, something that is much less common in non-human species. To explain this, Trivers developed the concept of reciprocal altruism (also simply known as reciprocation). Reciprocation consists of one individual providing aid to another in the 'expectation' that it will later receive aid in return.

There is a darker side to human sociality which can be seen in the in-group/out-group bias where we perceive and treat members of our own group more positively than those belonging to other groups. It has been used by social psychologists and sociologists to explain hostility between groups. Evolutionary psychologists suggest that this propensity arose via natural selection in order to promote group cohesion and cooperation to help repel attacks from other groups in our ancestral past, something that is known as parochial altruism.

Cooperation doesn't just happen, it needs to be motivated and, according to researchers such as Alan Fiske and Oliver Curry, this is what morality is for. Morality uses powerful emotions such as guilt, shame and pride to drive us towards engaging in reciprocal action. Moral transgressions leads others to punish, engaging in what Fiske and Rai describe as virtuous violence.

FURTHER READING

Stroebe, W. and Hewstone, M. (Eds) (2021) *An Introduction to Social Psychology*. Chichester: John Wiley & Sons.

Neuberg, S. L., Kenrick, D. T. and Schaller, M. (2010) Evolutionary social psychology. In S. T. Fiske, D. T. Gilbert and G. Lindzey (Eds.), *Handbook of Social Psychology*. Chichester: John Wiley & Sons, pp. 761–796.

Schaller, M., Simpson, J. A. and Kenrick, D. T. (2006) *Evolution and Social Psychology: Frontiers of Social Psychology*. New York: Psychology Press.

Fiske, A. P. and Rai, T. S. (2014) *Virtuous Violence: Hurting and Killing to Create, Sustain, End, and Honor Social Relationships*. Cambridge: Cambridge University Press.

4

EVOLUTION AND DEVELOPMENT

What is childhood for?

As we discussed in Chapter 1, evolutionary psychology asks ultimate questions as well as proximate ones. Proximate questions, remember, are questions about relatively recent causal mechanisms for a behaviour. We might ask what cognitive or neurobiological mechanisms underpin language, or what developmental factors influence personality development. Ultimate questions, on the other hand, ask why a particular behaviour or trait is there in the first place in terms of its effect on survival and reproduction. An example of this is disgust which is thought to exist to protect us from harmful pathogens that might cause disease (see Chapter 6). The question that begins this chapter – what is childhood for? – seems a strange question to ask, but from the point of view of evolution it is an important one. As you hopefully now realise, the process of natural selection is all about reproduction – if you don't reproduce evolution doesn't occur, so it seems somewhat strange that so many organisms spend so much time in a state where they are unable to reproduce (which is the definition of childhood). This is particularly the case for humans who often take 14 or 16 years to reach sexual maturity. From this perspective it seems like childhood is a waste of time, but it is worse than that as children are dependent upon their parents, which limits the number of children that they can have.

It might be tempting to think that this is simply the time it takes to grow a body from the size of a baby to the size of an adult. And it is true that human new-borns are very immature (Hrdy 2009). Some have even suggested that babies are born as much as 12

DOI: 10.4324/9780429274428-4

months premature (Martin 1990) this being the result of their large brains and the narrow pelvises of females that were re-engineered for bi-pedal locomotion. Unfortunately, this doesn't let us off the hook. For comparison, our closest relatives, the chimpanzees, reach sexual maturity at around seven years and even that is a long time compared to other large animals such as horses (around 12 months) and kangaroos (which have even more helpless babies than ours – hence the pouch) around 20 months.

We are faced with the conclusion that something is deliberately putting on the brakes and slowing down the process of sexual maturation in humans even more so than other animals and extending the period of childhood. But why? One answer is that human society is so complex that it takes many years to acquire the relevant cognitive and social skills to thrive within it, find a mate and effectively rear children of their own. Kuzawa, Chugani, Grossman, Lipovich, Muzik, Hof and Lange (2014) argue that the brain steals resources to grow itself that would otherwise be used to grow the body. But ultimately this is the same point at its root. The brain needs time and input in the form of experience so that it can effectively guide behaviour in the way that we have just described. We discuss this notion later in more detail including how our developing brains might be sensitive to their own particular environment and be able to adjust the process of development itself in order to maximise reproductive fitness.

Before we arrive at that heady place, we should spend a little time discussing how much behaviour is the result of genes and the environment, first focussing on the nature–nurture debate and then moving on to a more technical interpretation of this by discussing heritability and behavioural genetics.

NATURE, NURTURE AND EVOLUTION

The nature–nurture debate is one of the oldest debates in psychology. At its core it discusses the extent to which behaviour is the product of our genetic inheritance (nature) or our environment (nurture). Although the debate is often posed as an either/or question, it is better to think of it as a continuum with each making its own contribution and, as we shall see, interacting with each other.

WHAT IS NATURE?

Anyone who has observed a new-born baby may well come to the same conclusion as many psychologists such as Sigmund Freud and Jean Piaget, that nature really doesn't play a great role in development. New-borns have some basic reflexes such as the ability to suckle, cry and respond to light and sound, but other than that they are extremely helpless. So if nature is interpreted as meaning 'behaviours that you are born with' then it is game over, nurture surely wins.

But if we shift the focus of the nature–nurture debate from behaviour itself to *predispositions* to develop certain behaviours, then maybe we can rescue the nature side of the debate. Take puberty for example. Few would argue that puberty is *caused* by the environment, although it might certainly be influenced by it (see later). Rather puberty is the result of a set of biologically specified programs that cause the child to slowly turn into an adult and these processes are under genetic control (Choi and Yoo 2013). So just because something isn't present at birth does not mean it is entirely environmental. Rather than defining nature as referring to things that are present at birth, a better definition might be 'any trait that has its ultimate origins in the genes inherited from parents, whether or not that trait is present at birth'.

WHAT IS NURTURE?

The word 'nurture' comes from the same root as 'nurse' (meaning 'to care for'), and this interpretation is consistent with what many consider to be the most important part of environmental influence – the relationship between child and its primary caregivers (e. g. mum and dad). However, the way nurture is more typically used is to describe the entirety of the child's environment and would include social factors such as interactions with peers (as well as parents), physical traumas such as oxygen starvation at birth, any diseases that the child has had or any toxins that have been ingested, other factors many of which we almost certainly know nothing about at the moment. The environment, you see, is a very broad and complicated set of influences as it simply describes the set of causes that aren't genetic.

NATURE NURTURE: EXPLAINING SIMILARITIES AND DIFFERENCES

An important distinction that needs to be made is the extent to which we are attempting to explain differences between people or similarities. Much of developmental psychology focusses on explaining differences between people such as why some people are more intelligent than others, why some people go on to develop a mental illness and why some people are bold and others shy. As we shall see, there are evolutionary theories that attempt to explain individual differences (see also Chapter 6). Somewhat less frequently, developmentalists will focus on things that we all share such as how we acquire language, manage social interactions or develop a sense of morality. Again, there are evolutionary psychological theories for these too. But to begin with, let us consider the nature–nurture debate as it applies to differences by looking at research into a concept known as heritability.

HERITABILITY

The problem with trying to separate out nature and nurture is that there are so many confounds. Say we wanted to find out whether intelligence was down to the genes or the environment we could run a study – as many have – in which we look at correlations between the child's intelligence and that of their parents. Imagine that you find that there is a positive correlation: more intelligent children tend to have more intelligent parents. What can you conclude? In terms of the nature–nurture debate, the answer is – nothing. Parents provide their DNA to their children but, in most cases, they also provide some of their environment so we cannot know which is making the difference. Are children smart because they have inherited 'smart' genes from their parents? Or is it because they have been brought up in a 'smart' environment? Or is it some combination of the two? What we need is a way of separating out these two influences so that we can study each one separately.

Fortunately, situations do exist that enable us to separate out these two forces: identical twins and adoption. Identical or **monozygotic twins** are clones in the sense that (barring the odd mutation) they share 100 per cent of their genes. Identical twins are the product of a single fertilised egg which splits so that one individual becomes two. Non-identical, fraternal or **dizygotic twins,** are the product of two eggs each fertilised by a separate sperm. They therefore share 50 per cent of their genes by common descent, just like regular siblings. These natural experiments provide the bedrock of a discipline known as **behavioural genetics** which, as the name suggests, attempts to estimate the effect that genes have on specific behaviours such as schizophrenia, personality or intelligence.

Because identical twins share twice as many genes on average as non-identical twins we can, using some quite complicated statistics, get an estimate as to the relative contribution of genes and the environment. If we find that identical twins are more similar on some trait than non-identical twins, then we have some evidence that genes are responsible, at least in part, for the existence of that trait.

Adoption similarly allows us to separate out nature and nurture. The kind of adoption that is studied by scientists is where two

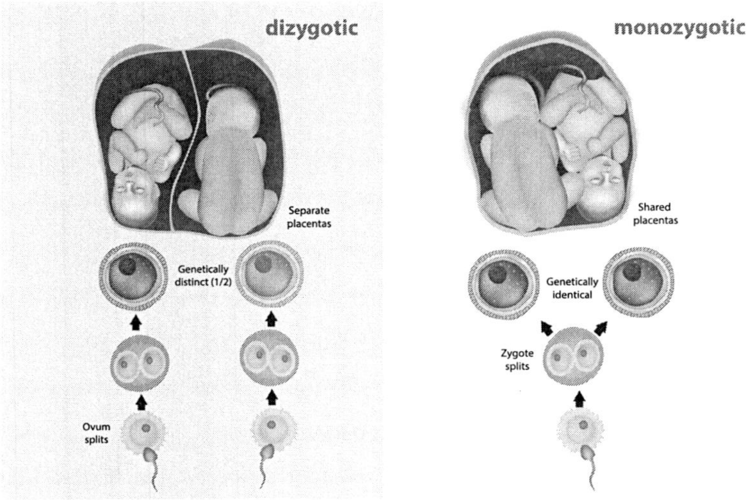

Figure 4.1 Monozygotic (right) and dizygotic (left) twins in the womb. Note that, due to arising from a single fertilised egg, monozygotic twins share all of their genes whereas dizygotic twins arise from two eggs leading to them sharing half of their genes by common descent

parents adopt two or more children – ideally from birth – who are genetically unrelated to each other. By comparing these adopted siblings to one another on some trait, we can get some estimate of, among other things, how much being in the same family influences the development of that trait: are these siblings more similar to one another than those raised in different families?

ESTIMATING HERITABILITY

Heritability it is the extent to which variation across different individuals is accounted for by genetic differences and it provides a number between 0 (no effect of genes) to 1 (no effect of the environment). So if we say that a trait has a heritability of .5 (or 50 per cent) we can state that the trait is half the result of genes and half the result of the environment. Note, however, that this is across many individuals; it is a statistical average and does not mean that for any one person 50 per cent of the trait is due to their genes and 50 per cent due to the environment. For example, it is generally accepted that height is around .8 (or 80 per cent) heritable (Yang, et al. 2010) so if you are 2 metres tall it doesn't mean that 160 cm of your height was caused by your genes and 40 cm by the environment.

To understand heritability, we first need to think about **concordance**. If we take a pair of twins then concordance is the extent to which the two twins are correlated on some trait. For example, to measure the concordance for intelligence we take a sample of twins (both monozygotic and dizygotic), give each twin an IQ test, and then look at the extent to which the scores correlate across pairs of twins. If we find that the correlation is higher for identical twins than for non-identical twins then we can assume that there is some genetic contribution for IQ; it is shared genes that is making the identical twins more similar. On the other hand, if we find that there is no difference in the correlation between identical and non-identical twins, then we can assume that genes are having no effect and intelligence is entirely environmental. To take a real-world example, for **autism spectrum disorder** the **concordance rate** is around 77 per cent for identical twins and 31 per cent for non-identical twins, suggesting that there is a strong, but not perfect genetic contribution (Hallmayer et al. 2011).

To make things a little simpler, these two concordance figures can be combined to provide a single number, which is known as the heritability coefficient. The method of calculating this is beyond the scope of this book, but if you do the sums, the concordance rates for autism discussed above yield a heritability estimate that .66, or 66 per cent of the variation in autism across Hallmayer's sample is accounted for by genes.

Behavioural geneticists can further partition environmental influence into two components: the **shared environment** and the **non-shared** or **unique** environment. The shared environment is the effect on the child of growing up in the same family and would include social economic status, parents' child rearing practices, or other common experiences such as at school. The non-shared environment relates to events that happened to one child but not the other. One child was bullied, the other was not; one child had a long-term illness, the other was healthy.

Calculating the effects of the shared and non-shared is complex and non-intuitive so, as before, we will sidestep that maths and return to the effects of the shared and non-shared environment shortly.

The early days of research on identical twins reared in different households produced some startling results. A pair of twins known as 'the Jim twins' were adopted from birth by families in different parts of the United States and were reunited at the age of 39, having never met one another. Their list of similarities is quite striking. Both had married and divorced women named Linda; had second marriages with women named Betty; had police training and worked part time with law enforcement agencies; had childhood pets they named Toy; had identical drinking and smoking patterns and had first-born sons named James Alan. Perhaps more famously there were the twins Jack and Oskar. Jack was raised by a Jewish family in Trinidad, Oskar by a German Catholic Nazi family. When they met as adults they discovered that both flushed the toilet before and after going, enjoyed sneezing in elevators to startle people, dipped buttered toast in coffee, wore rubber bands on their wrists and hated floral centrepiece displays on tables (apparently because it obstructed the view of other people opposite).

WHAT THE DATA TELLS US ABOUT NATURE–NURTURE AND INDIVIDUAL DIFFERENCES

So which traits are heritable, and which are not? Rather shockingly it seems that they all are. Or at least all of the ones that have been investigated. This is sometimes known as Turkheimer's first law: 'all human behavioural traits are heritable' (Turkheimer 2000). While this might be a little overstated, it is surprising how many traits seem to have at least some degree of heritability. Most personality traits (extraversion, neuroticism, openness to experience, conscientiousness and agreeableness) have heritabilities of around .5, meaning that 50 per cent of the variation among people is due to genes. Intelligence is a little higher with about .7 heritability (70 per cent). Even behaviours apparently unrelated to genes are heritable. Voting behaviour, for example (Fowler, Baker and Dawes 2008), suggests that genes account for at least some of the variation in political affiliation. On the face of it this seems odd; political parties didn't exist in our evolutionary past so how might our genes account for our political beliefs? An answer is that many of the principles that underlie different political perspectives derive from individual differences in personality. For example, research suggests that people who score highly on openness to experience are more likely to be left-leaning, whereas those who are higher in conscientiousness tend to lean more towards the right (Krieger, Becker, Greiff and Spinath 2019).

Turkheimer's second law, 'the effect of being raised in the same family is smaller than the effect of the genes', relates to the shared and non-shared environment discussed above. Research suggests that unrelated children who are adopted and brought up as siblings in the same family environment are no more similar to each other than any two unrelated children chosen at random from the population (see, for example, Plomin and Daniels 1987). The measures in these studies were the heritability of personality, cognitive skills and mental illness. At most, the data suggest that the shared environment accounts for 10 per cent of variation among people (Turkheimer 2000). Whatever effect families have on children, it doesn't seem to make them more similar to each other, at least in the measures that were taken for this study.

Turkheimer's third and final law is, 'A substantial portion of the variation in complex human behavioural traits is not accounted for by the effects of genes or families'. This relates to the non-shared environment. In studies on many different kinds of trait, this is by far the largest environmental contributor to how children turn out, rivalling, and in some cases exceeding the effect of the genes. As a rough estimate, and averaging over many studies and traits, Turkheimer suggests that genes account for 40–50 per cent of variation, the shared environment around 10 per cent and the remaining 50 per cent being the result of the shared or unique environment.

Are you surprised by this? Well you probably should be because what it means is that growing up in the same household does not make children more similar to each other than if they grew up in entirely different households. Indeed, behavioural geneticist Robert Plomin points out that children who were adopted at birth resemble their biological parents almost as closely as if they had grown up with them.

BOX 4.1 GENE ENVIRONMENT INTERACTIONS

First, consider that children who grow up with their biological parents are going to inherit some of their parents' traits, but are also going to grow up in a household environment that reflects their parents' dispositions. Thus, intelligent parents will pass genes for intelligence on to their offspring but will also create an 'intelligent' environment for their children, replete with books and ballet lessons. This double whammy is called a passive gene–environment interaction.

Second, consider that how you appear and behave affects how people treat you. Friendly people tend to be liked, rude people disliked, quiet people ignored. Rude people more than likely live in a world surrounded by people who act in a hostile way towards them as a response to their rudeness. If we further imagine that rudeness is heritable (and it almost certainly is, see Turkheimer's law above) then we can see that how people treat the person is an indirect effect of their genes. This hostility is likely to make them even ruder, creating a vicious circle in which traits become more entrenched and stronger because the environment reinforces the traits that were initially caused by genes. This is a so-called reactive or evocative gene–environment interaction.

Finally, consider that people tend to seek out people who are like them and activities that satisfy them. So thrill-seekers hang out with other thrill-seekers and enjoy BASE jumping and other risky activities, again reinforcing the effects of the genes. This is called an active gene–environment interaction.

In these three examples we can see that the genes and the environment are acting together to reinforce a particular kind of behaviour, but in behavioural genetic studies because the behaviours are correlated with genes they would all be put down as effects of the genes (or more strictly the effects of the effects of the genes), even though the environment is playing a role.

HOW HERITABILITY CAN MISLEAD

Finally, we must add a cautionary tale about behavioural genetics. Consider the example given by geneticist Richard Lewontin (1970). Lewontin asks us to imagine that we buy a normal packet of seeds from the garden centre which, as is typical, will all be genetically different from one another. We then plant the seeds in two pots (see Figure 4.2); one pot receives normal concentration of nutrients, while the other is deficient. If someone were to ask the question 'why are some plants taller than others, is it nature or is it nurture?', the answer depends upon which plants you are discussing. If we are asking why some of the plants within a particular pot are taller than others within the same pot, then the answer is that it is down to genes. The environment is the same for all plants within a pot, so the only possible source of variation is genetic. On the other hand, if we mean why are the plants in one pot on average taller than the plants in the other pot then the answer is that it is environment. Given that we randomly allocated the seeds to the pots, there is no reason to suspect that there is any net genetic difference between the two pots, so it is almost certainly the difference between the two environments (nutrients) that is causing the difference.

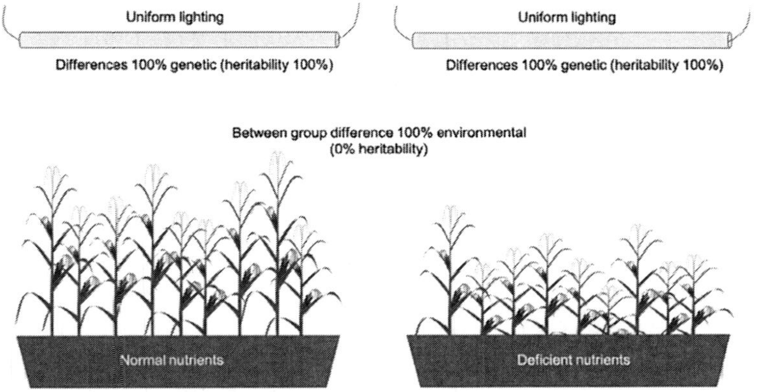

Figure 4.2 Richard Lewontin's plant-based thought experiment (redrawn by authors)

You might be wondering what this has to do with development. Quite a lot, as a matter of fact. Imagine that the pots are schools and the plants are children within those schools and instead of height we are measuring educational achievement. If we ask the question, 'why are some children doing better than others?', an analysis within an individual school might reveal that the differences between children were largely genetic, which, if taken seriously by policy makers, might lead them to the conclusion that there is no point in investing in teachers as 'it is all in the genes'. A study that compared one school to another might, as we have seen, reveal the importance of the environment in educational achievement and thereby recommend investing in teaching resources. This salutary lesson is by no means meant to undermine the importance of behavioural genetics research, it is to point out that like all research, one needs to be careful about how one interprets it.

BOX 4.2 HOW MANY GENES? GENOME-WIDE ASSOCIATION STUDIES

If you've read other chapters of this book, you will know about the idea that behavioural traits such as personality and intelligence are the result of many genes, rather than just one. The hope of, for example, finding a gene for schizophrenia was always a hopeless enterprise and research has borne this out. But if not one gene, then how many? No one really knew, until a technique known as genome-wide association studies was developed. Abbreviated to GWAS (pronounced Gee Wass), such studies take a large number of people (frequently thousands) showing the trait of interest, schizophrenia, say, and a similarly large number of people without the target trait who form the control condition. Sequencing techniques are then used to determine the genetic make-up of each participant (their genome), which are then submitted for a powerful statistical analysis. In essence, researchers are trying to find what genes are present in the target group that are not present in the control group. Technically these differences will be variants of 'normal' genes called alleles or, even more technically, Single-Nucleotide Polymorphisms or SNPS (pronounced 'snips'). The results of this research are startling. For most complex traits such as schizophrenia or bipolar disorder, the number of differences runs into the thousands. Given that so many genes are associated with such disorders, it is perhaps unsurprising that the symptoms that people experience can be quite variable where people might have schizophrenic-like symptoms without experiencing the full-blown illness. And, of course, that is without considering the effects of the environment.

LIFE HISTORY THEORY AND DEVELOPMENT

Although not perfect, behavioural genetics really is the gold-standard in understanding the relative contributions of genes and the environment to development. However, from an evolutionary point of view it answers proximate questions about the causal mechanisms for individual differences rather than ultimate questions about what the function of these individual differences might be. This is not a criticism of behavioural genetics because that is not what it was designed to do, but as evolutionists we need to be continually asking ourselves the 'why' question.

And behavioural genetics is not alone in not asking why – the overwhelming majority of theories in developmental psychology fail to ask this important question. Take attachment theory. Attachment theory attempts to explain how adults and children relate to each other by tracing their experiences back to the very earliest relationship with their primary caregiver. If the primary caregiver was psychologically or physically absent, then the child is said to respond by developing an **insecure avoidant** attachment style where they find it difficult to get close to people. At the opposite end of the continuum inconsistent parenting in which children are given too much love at some times and too little at others would lead to **insecure anxious-resistant** (sometimes called **anxious-ambivalent**) attachment. These people are continually worried that they will lose the people they love, leading to them monitoring the other person and becoming anxious that they will leave them. Parents who manage to strike the happy medium produce children who are in the Goldilocks zone (neither too much nor too little) and are described as having **secure attachments** (there are other forms of attachment style but these are the basic three).

These attachment styles have implications for future relationship success with securely attached individuals tending to have more stable, longer-term relationships, anxious-resistant individuals having more fractious and volatile relationships and insecure avoidant individuals having less intimate, more superficial relationships. The latter also tend to have more sexual partners, more relationship breakdowns and show an interest in sex earlier than either of the other two groups (Shaver and Hazan 1987).

One of the many puzzles about research into attachment is that around 35 per cent of children and adults are classified as having one of the insecure attachment styles, which is very high if one thinks, as is often implied, that these attachment styles are dysfunctional. Might it be that, at the level of the gene, insecure attachments are in some ways adaptive? Or, in other words, why?

LIFE HISTORY THEORY AND ATTACHMENT

At its core, life history theory is a theory of where resources should be allocated during development and during reproduction. In developmental terms resources such as energy and effort can be directed towards growing our bodies (somatic effort) or in reproduction (reproductive effort). In the best of all possible worlds we would maximise both, but in the real world there are always trade-offs, resources are limited and resources that go into one cannot go into the other. What should you choose? As always, the answer is 'it depends'. Risk seems to be an important factor. It is pretty pointless devoting effort to building a strong and healthy body if the likelihood of death from external factors such as predation are going to end your life before you get the opportunity to reproduce. Or, alternatively, think of it from the genes' perspective. As we alluded to at the beginning of this chapter, children (or juveniles if we are discussing other animals) are a prison for their genes because the only way that genes can effectively leave the organism is via the reproductive process. So life history theory assumes that genes have in some ways created bodies (and brains) that are sensitive to risk; a risky environment, the theory predicts, should see a shift of emphasis from somatic effort to reproductive effort where the interest is in early maturation and early reproduction.

From a parenting perspective there is a similar trade-off. In risk-free environments it might make sense to have relatively few offspring and devote time and energy to bringing them up, but it makes no sense at all to do this if there is a high likelihood that they will all die, or be killed before they reach maturity. This tends to be the pattern – that we find some organisms have a slow life history where they develop slowly and have fewer offspring that they invest in heavily (mammals obviously), whereas others have a fast life history where maturation happens briskly and emphasis is placed on having a large number of offspring with little or no investment. Many fish and insects do this (Wilson and MacArthur 2016).

Psychologist Jay Belsky (1999) inspected the results of attachment research through the lens of life history theory and concluded that the difference between secure and insecure-avoidant strategies could be explained by sensitivity to riskiness. Recall that some of the characteristics of insecure-avoidant include reproducing earlier, having more children by more partners, having more divorce and relationship breakdowns (Shaver and Hazan 1987), which are the kinds of patterns we might expect if the strategy that they are playing is focussed on reproduction rather than somatic growth.

BOX 4.3 A LIFE HISTORY ACCOUNT OF PLAY

Many young animals, especially mammals, engage in play and for centuries there were debates as to what this apparently functionless activity was for. Why should it be for anything? Well, from an evolutionary perspective, organisms that spend time and energy engaged in pointless activities should suffer (in terms of natural selection) compared to those that use their time and energy judiciously. The consensus now is that play, far from being pointless, is a vital part of development. Juveniles are, in fact, practising the skills that will become useful in adulthood but in a safe environment: kittens play at hunting, young male chimpanzees play at fighting and so on. According to life history theory, then, play is an activity designed to maximise future reproductive success because its benefits will only be realised later on down the line.

Figure 4.3 Brown bear cubs, like humans, engage in play
Source: www.shutterstock.com/image-photo/brown-bear-cups-playing-lake-national-105013313

But the extent to which an animal engages in play is conditional upon environmental conditions. When riskiness is high, animals play less (Fagen 1977), presumably because they are spending time engaged in activities that maximise current reproductive success. Not only can risky environments lead to lower levels of play they, can change the kind of play that the animal engages in. Bateson, Mendl and Feaver (1990) found that female cats that were on a restricted diet weaned their offspring more quickly than those on normal diets. This is to be expected as the cats want to discharge their burden of childcare as quickly as possible under poor conditions – they are maximising current reproductive fitness. Once weaned, their offspring play, in fact they play more than the offspring of cats on normal diets, but the play is different as they spend more time practising hunting – which is important if they are to achieve independence – at the expense of social play which is associated with more long-term goals of reproduction and childcare.

Further research shows that indicators of environmental riskiness are associated with early sexual maturity in girls. Belsky, Houts and Fearon (2010) found that 65 per cent of girls categorised as insecure-avoidant at 15 months of age experienced menarche (onset of puberty) at less than 10.5 years of age compared with 54 per cent of those categorised as secure at the same age. Belsky et al. (2010) found that girls whose mothers treated them harshly when they were 15 months of age became sexually mature earlier, as before, but also showed greater sexual risk-taking when they were adolescents.

Measurement of maternal harshness was achieved by the responses that their mothers gave to a questionnaire – harshness being measured by agreeing that spanking is a reasonable punishment for wrongdoing, believing that children should respect authority, be quiet when adults are around, and the feeling that praise and hugs 'spoil' the child.

Risky environments are also associated with early pregnancy. A study by Nettle, Coal and Dickens (2011) of 4,553 women in the United Kingdom found that early pregnancy was associated with environmental risk factors such as low birth weight, short duration of breastfeeding, separation from mother in childhood, frequent family residential moves and lack of paternal involvement. These associations remained when they controlled for socio-economic status and the age of the respondents' mothers when they gave birth.

So harshness of various kinds seems to increase the likelihood of a fast life history including pubertal timing of girls; but what about boys? Research shows that there is little effect of harshness on boys' pubertal timing (Belsky et al. 2007), although as boys don't experience menarche, it is more difficult to determine when puberty starts. But there is research showing that harshness affects other traits such as number of partners, early interest in sex and so on (Chang et al. 2019).

This is merely a sample of what has become a very productive and popular area of research over the past ten years or so. What is interesting about the application of life history theory to development is that it provides an ultimate answer as to why different attachment styles exist. It argues that displaying avoidant attachment styles is not dysfunctional, rather it is an adaptive response to living in a harsh environment where individuals might not be able to rely on a stable future or even a future at all. There is still much work to do as biologists have criticised the psychological use of life history theory for not containing any formal modelling to confirm its predictions (see Nettle and Frankenhuis 2020). But if the application of life history theory to psychological development is correct, it shows that development is much more nuanced and adaptive than we used to think it was.

EXPLORING SIMILARITIES BETWEEN PEOPLE: THE CASE OF COGNITIVE DEVELOPMENT

Jean Piaget was probably the first person to take seriously the problem of cognitive development. The question that he worked on for most of his long life was how do apparently unintelligent babies become intelligent adults? Piaget believed that one of the most important tasks that the new-born faced was developing what he called the 'object concept'. This is the understanding that physical objects are enduring entities that exist independently of the infant's ability to perceive them. According to Piaget, this is not developed fully until the child reaches around 18 months of age, when they leave the **sensorimotor period** and move into the **pre-operational period**. Piaget's evidence for this is that children younger than 18 months fail to search for a desirable object such as a brightly coloured toy if it is obscured by an opaque screen.

Piaget's proposal that infants know next to nothing about the physical world is a curious one from an evolutionary standpoint. Humans and their ancestors have had millions of years dealing with physical objects so it is odd that evolution did not give humans and their ancestors a head start by wiring such information into their brains.

Piaget believed that children go through several revolutions in the way that they think about the world, which he described as developmental stages or periods (the distinction need not concern us). Piaget believed that the very youngest children from 0 to around 18 months of age are said to be in the sensorimotor period and have no understanding of objects as enduring entities. For them objects only exist for as long as they can be perceived and once out of sight no longer exist. As the child grows older they gradually begin to understand that objects exist independent of their ability to see them, known as object permanence. At this point, they are said to be in the pre-operational period (18 months to 7 years, approx.). In this stage children have an unusual – to us adults – understanding of matter which leads to them believing that the amount of 'stuff' (say liquid or modelling clay) can be changed simply by changing its shape (e.g. pouring liquid from a tall, narrow glass into a short, wide one changes the amount of water). This is known as a failure to conserve, and the experiments to show this are Piaget's famous conservation tasks.

Once a child is able to conserve, they are said to be in the **concrete operational period** (approximately 7–11 years of age) where they have a good understanding of the physical world but have difficulty with logic and abstraction. These are not fully mastered until the child enters the formal operational period at around 11 years.

DO BABIES HAVE OBJECT PERMANENCE?

In the 1990s Renee Baillargeon (Baillargeon 1987) devised the apparatus depicted in Figure 4.3 which was specifically designed to test for object permanence in infants. Babies of 3–4 months of age are seated in front of an apparatus in which a screen slowly rotates through 180 degrees away from them. Babies are initially fascinated by the screen and spend time staring at it. After a time, they become bored and start to look away. At this point the screen stops and a block is placed behind the screen. At this point one of two things happens, depending on experimental conditions. In one sequence of events the screen rotates and stops at 112 degrees from the horizontal as if it had hit the now out of sight block (the possible event). In another condition the screen rotates through the full 180 degrees *as if the block was not there* (the impossible event).

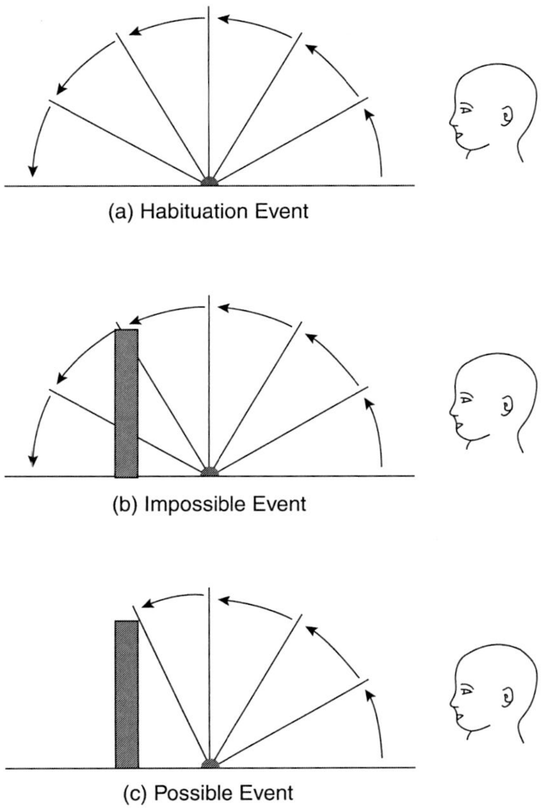

Figure 4.4 The apparatus used by Baillargeon

If Piaget were correct, and babies of 3–4 months have no sense of object permanence then, at the point at which the screen obscures the block, the baby should think the object has popped out of existence and should therefore carry on its merry way to the full 180 degrees. On the other hand, if they *did* have object permanence, then they would find this surprising – 'where's that block gone?' – where surprise is measured by the amount of time that babies spend looking at the screen. Baillargeon found that, just like adults, 3–4 months old babies spend more time looking at the impossible event than the possible event suggesting, that they understand that the block is still there, even when it cannot be seen.

So babies seem to acquire object permanence much earlier in their lives than Piaget believed, as would be expected if evolution had given them a head start in understanding the physical world. And the more infant cognition is taken seriously, the more competent they appear. Other research has shown that young babies understand that 1+1 = 2 and that 2–1 = 1 (Wynn 1995), that objects cannot pass through one another or occupy the same physical space as another object, that an object passing from A to B has to pass through all of the points in between and that objects cannot influence one another without physical contact. These last three findings were discovered by Spelke, Breinlinger, Macomber and Jacobson (1992). Note than none of this evidence conclusively shows that any of these physical principles are innate because they are all shown by babies of around three or four months, not new-borns. What it does show is that such principles at least develop much more quickly than was previously thought, suggesting that they may be supported by innate principles. Other research has shown that new-borns have particular competences, including a preference for faces (Morton and Johnson 1991) a preference for language-like sounds (Kuhl et al. 1992) and a preference – at birth! – for the rhythms and sounds of their mother tongue (Moon, Lagercrantz and Kuhl 2013), suggesting that some aspects of language are being learned before the baby is even born.

The evidence from developmental psychology therefore shows that, although humans are not born with a complete knowledge of the physical and social world, they do seem to come equipped with psychological dispositions that serve to focus their attention on the evolutionary meaningful stimuli to enable them to learn about the world much more rapidly than if they were relying on trial and error alone.

SUMMARY

Research in development has been dominated by the nature–nurture debate, with researchers typically emphasising the importance of one over the other. By using twin and adoption studies, researchers are able to estimate the unique contribution of genes and the environment to the development of a wide range of traits. Looking at individual differences in development using behavioural genetics shows that nature and nurture both have a role to play in many behaviours. But it is important to understand the limitations of such research.

Behavioural genetics does not provide any ultimate explanation for why we see individual differences in behaviour but life history theory does. Life history theory claims that developing children are sensitive to environmental factors such as riskiness and harshness and are able to fine-tune their developmental trajectory accordingly. The example we discussed, the existence of avoidant attachment styles, viewed through the lens of life history theory, is not dysfunctional, but rather an adaptive response to a risky environment.

Although young babies are relatively helpless compared to those of other primates, recent research suggests that there is a lot going on beneath the surface. Babies seem to have innate predispositions to understand many aspects of the world, which directs their attention towards relevant stimuli and gives them a head-start in understanding the way that the world works.

FURTHER READING

Belsky, J., Caspi, A., Moffitt, T. E. and Poulton, R. (2020) *The Origins of You: How Childhood Shapes Later Life*. Cambridge, MA: Harvard University Press.

Gopnik, A., Meltzoff, A. N. and Kuhl, P. K. (2001) *How Babies Think: The Science of Childhood*. London: Phoenix. (An excellent introduction to some of the recent work on cognitive development.)

Plomin, R. (2019) *Blueprint, with a New Afterword: How DNA Makes Us Who We Are*. Cambridge, MA: MIT Press.

5

THINKING AND FEELING
COGNITION AND EMOTIONS

COGNITION AND EMOTION: TWO THINGS OR ONE?

One of the fundamental divisions in psychology is that between thought and the emotions. Thought is seen as rational, cool-headed, and emotions as irrational, hot-headed and 'passionate' (in past times emotions were referred to as 'the passions'). Although this distinction dates back to the Ancient Greek philosophers, the separation of the rational and the emotional is usually attributed to the French philosopher René Descartes. In this chapter we discuss cognition and emotion and reflect upon whether it makes sense to keep them separate in the way that tradition has dictated.

WHAT IS COGNITION?

Psychologists use the word 'cognition' to describe the process of thinking (the term cognition comes from the Latin word *cogito*, which means 'to think'). But cognition is something that is much broader than the kind of conscious, deliberate activity that we often associate with thought. For example, in addition to conscious thought, cognitive psychologists also study unconscious, automatic processes such as those that underlie vision or language processing. Cognitive scientists therefore describe cognition as being anything that involves *information processing*. This is a very broad term which can include the processing of information coming in from the senses, such as vision, which can be processed in order to render a three-dimensional model of the world (we discuss vision later). It might also involve retrieving information that has been stored in

DOI: 10.4324/9780429274428-5

memory in response to an external stimulus, e.g. remembering that a particular food is tasty. It also involves the storing of new information, e.g. that a food has made you sick and should therefore be avoided.

This last case is very powerful. Food or drink that makes you sick, especially if it is unfamiliar to you, can lead to a very powerful aversion to consuming that substance again, as many people might well know if they have had the unfortunate experience of being sick after drinking a strong-tasting alcoholic beverage. Often just thinking about it can make you feel queasy. Interestingly, but perhaps not surprisingly, this is something we share with many other organisms.

This means that cognition is so much more than conscious thought. In fact, we can apply its principles to all types of information processing systems, from explaining the behaviour of a computer to the behaviour of a single-celled organism, such as an amoeba.

WHAT IS EMOTION?

We consider emotion in further detail later but in general we can define an emotion as a specific state an organism enters into as a response to particular internal or external conditions in order to promote an adaptive behavioural outcome. For example, a threat to an organism's life or wellbeing is likely to lead to it entering into a state which leads to it removing itself from the threat. We might label such a state as 'fear'. In contrast, the need for sustenance or other important resources might lead it to explore the environment. We might label such a state as 'curiosity'. Such various states are accompanied by psychological and physiological changes, including a change in heart rate, focussing on attentional, and in some organisms such as humans, visual changes in bodily or facial expressions.

WHY WE NEED BOTH COGNITION AND EMOTION

In science fiction, there are many creatures that seem to have no emotion at all. Indeed, in *Doctor Who* the Cybermen claim that emotions are a weakness and Mr Spock from the original series of

Star Trek was also rigidly unemotional. So, are emotions a weakness and, if not, what benefits do they bring?

Consider fear. Imagine a hungry animal that has just settled down to eat some tasty morsel of food when suddenly a predator appears. A purely cognitive animal might weigh up the pros and cons of running away and saving its life against its need to eat but that might take up precious seconds that make the difference between life or death.

Having a fear response means that the animal is rapidly put into a state that increases vigilance, and this affects cognition; the animal is now focussing all of its attention on the predator – it is, perhaps, retrieving information from past experience about how the predator might strike, in order to flee in an appropriate manner. There are also physiological consequences such as increasing blood sugar levels for energy and the diversion of blood from non-essential processes, such as digestion, to the muscles that facilitate fight or flight. The animal is like the coiled spring. The predator strikes, but its prey is gone.

Cognition and emotion therefore work together. Cognitive processes such as vision (seeing another animal) and memory (identifying this animal as dangerous) lead to emotional responses (fear), which itself has consequences on subsequent cognition.

So, emotions are most definitely not a weakness; they are a vital contributor to our survival. Cognition and emotion may be different systems, but they work together closely with one informing the other. So, let's spend some time considering cognition in more detail.

COGNITION?

Prior to the development of cognitive psychology, the dominant approach to psychology in the United States and in Europe was **behaviourism**. Its chief advocate at the time, B.F. Skinner, argued that we should focus only on stimuli (e.g. appearance of a predator) and behaviour (e.g. animal fights or flees) and should not consider what happens in between. This became known as the **black box** approach because it explicitly ignores such mental processing. Skinner's rationale for this was that the mind contains entities such as ideas, beliefs and feelings, and none of these – in his view at least – are capable of being objectively measured and are therefore unable to be scientifically scrutinised.

The early cognitive psychologists, including such figures as, Donald Broadbent, Herbert Simon, Alan Newell, George Miller thought differently. They drew their inspiration from the rapid development of digital computers during the 1950s because they noted strong similarities between the computer and the mind. Both took in information, processed that information, and had the capacity to store the results of that processing if necessary.

While cognitive psychology has developed a great deal since the 1950s, the broad approach remains the same. That is, to understand the mind as an information processing system. In recent years one important advance has been the development of a range of **neuroimaging** techniques, which allow for a glimpse inside the black box.

BOX 5.1 NEUROIMAGING

Brain-scanning technology has enabled researchers to see what is happening in the brain. Examples include PET (positron emission tomography), CAT (computer axial tomography), MRI (magnetic resonance imaging), fMRI (functional magnetic resonance imaging) and MEG (magnetoencephalography). The last two are particularly important as they enable the brain's activity to be monitored over time as it changes in response to a stimulus. If you like, it is a video of the brain's activity. The others present a photographic snap shot of the brain as it processes stimuli. These neuroimaging techniques work in various different ways. CAT (or CT) scans work by firing an enormous number of x-rays from a wide range of angles through the brain. The information from these is then assembled to produce 3D images.

PET scans involve the drinking of a solution containing radioactive glucose which emits positively charged electrons (known as positrons). During the performance of a cognitive task, the regions of the brain which are particularly active make a greater use of this radioactive glucose, and the positrons emitted are detected by sensors enabling researchers to determine which areas of the brain are most active.

MRI, fMRI and MEG rely on the fact that oxygenated and deoxygenated haemoglobin have different magnetic properties. Using sensitive detectors these differences can be detected enabling the degree of blood flow in the brain to be measured and thus determine which parts of the brain are more active on a specific cognitive task.

Another recently developed method (not strictly speaking neuroimaging but nonetheless important) is Transcranial Magnetic Stimulation (TMS). TMS makes use of powerful magnets to stimulate certain areas of the brain while researchers observe the effects on behaviour. TMS is also used sometimes to 'shut down' some brain regions to create the equivalent of a temporary stroke like-effect.

EVOLUTION AND COGNITION

The main focus of cognitive psychology is focused on proximate questions such as *how* we solve something, rather than ultimate questions such as *why* we solve something in a particular way. Evolutionary cognitive psychologists have begun to consider why the mind processes information in the way that it does. An example of this can be seen in the study of visual illusions.

EVOLUTION AND THE VISUAL SYSTEM

Have a look at the picture in Figure 5.1a (from Adelson, 2000).

You probably won't believe this but the squares labelled A and B are exactly the same shade of grey. Proof is given in Figure 5.1b.

Astonishingly, the two vertical lines are exactly the same shade throughout their length (cover up the rest of the picture if you find this hard to believe), yet each line blends in perfectly with the two squares. This might be taken to suggest our visual system is poorly designed, in the sense that it is creating differences (in this case of shade) that aren't objectively out there in the real world. This, however, raises the question as to what the visual system was designed *for*.

The British neuroscientist and psychologist David Marr (1982) was perhaps the first person to consider the function of the visual

Figure 5.1a Are the squares A and B the same shade of grey or different?

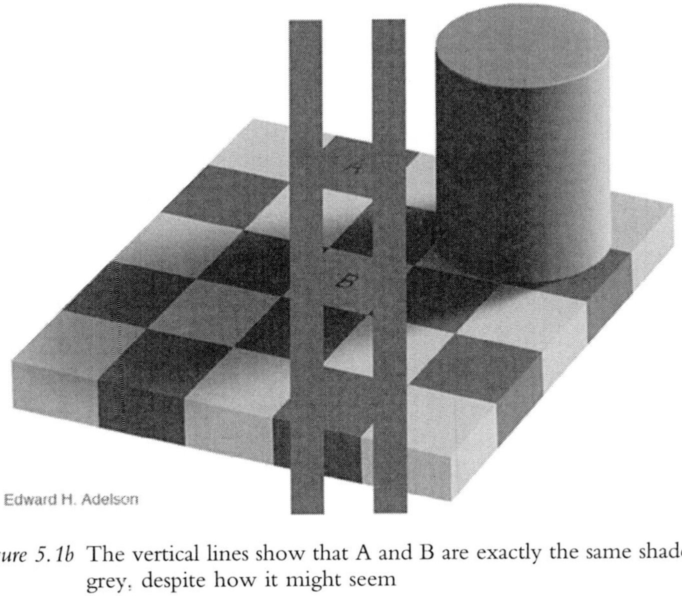

Figure 5.1b The vertical lines show that A and B are exactly the same shade of grey, despite how it might seem

system. The obvious answer is, of course, to see, but what are we actually seeing? How does what we see relate to what is out there in the visual world?

This is why visual illusions such as that in Figure 5.1 are so useful. They reveal that what we see is somewhat different from what is out there. Marr's leap was that some of these illusions show that the visual system is, in fact, *well* designed. To see why, look again at Figure 5.1. What you perceive is a chessboard 'floor' of squares of two shades with a shadow falling across it. If, however, your visual system accurately reproduced the light intensities arriving at the retina, it would look like a chessboard pattern with squares all of various different shades (look at the shades at the edges, they are different to the surfaces, for example), and if the shadow were to move it would appear that the squares were changing as it passed over them. The effect would be that, as lighting conditions changed, the world would change dramatically from moment to moment. So, this bug, as software engineers are apt to say, is actually a feature. The visual system is able to create a stable world despite there being constant changes in luminosity.

Why might the visual system be designed in this way? The answer is because most of the time changes in luminance aren't important. What is important is that we detect real objects, which we might stumble over, or which might signal food or threats; we don't want to have our attention continually drawn to 'ghosts' or shadows. Hence, our visual system is designed by natural selection to provide us with information in order to make decisions about how to act in an ever-changing environment.

EVOLUTIONARY EXPLANATIONS OF LOGICAL FALLACIES

In 1966 psychologist Peter Wason was interested in the extent to which people could reason in a logical manner. In one study he presented participants with four cards with either letters or numbers on them (see Figure 5.2) and told them that if a card had a letter on one side it would have a number on the other and vice versa. They were then given the following rule:

> IF there is a vowel on one side of the card, THEN there is an even number on the other.

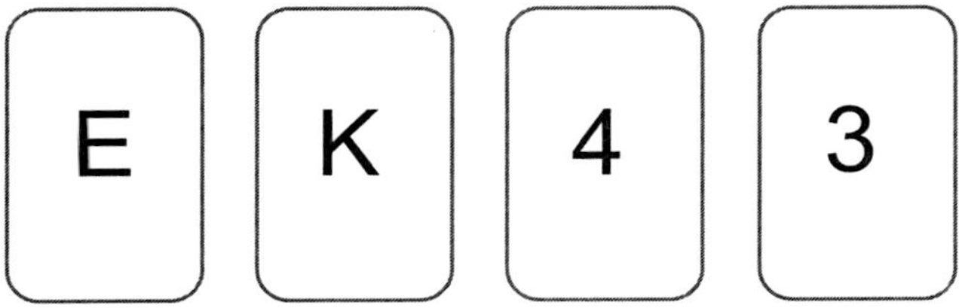

Figure 5.2 Stimuli cards used by Wason (1966)

Participants were then asked to point to all the cards that are capable of breaking this rule.

Consider this problem for a moment: which cards would you choose and how many?

Let us consider each card in turn. The first card is an 'E' which is a vowel. If you were to turn that card over and found an even number it would conform to the rule, but if it had an odd number, it would break the rule, so definitely turn over the 'E' card. The next card is a 'K' which is a consonant, and the rule says nothing about consonants so the rule cannot be broken. The '4' card looks tempting as the rule mentions even numbers, but if on turning it over you find a vowel, then that is in accordance with the rule, if it is a consonant it doesn't apply, as before. The final card is an odd number and on turning this card over, should we find a vowel, then the rule is broken. So the correct answers are 'E' and '3'.

In the original study only 4 per cent chose 'E' and '3'. Most (46 per cent) chose 'E' and '4' and 33 per cent chose 'E' on its own. Things don't get much better if we use real words rather than letters and numbers. Manktelow and Evans (1979) presented participants with the statement, 'every time I eat haddock then I drink gin', and then gave them cards 'haddock', 'cod', 'gin' and 'whisky', and found no improvement.

Things were very much improved by a study conducted by Griggs and Cox (1982). In one version of their task participants were given the rule 'If a person is drinking alcohol THEN they must be over the age of 18', and given cards that contained the words 'Beer', 'Coke', '21', '17'.

If you are like the participants in the study you probably found this much easier, with around 74 per cent of people choosing the correct cards. We can see that the 'Beer' card could break the rule if on the other side is a number smaller than 18. The 'Coke' card, like the consonant card, is irrelevant – 21-year-olds can drink alcohol so they cannot break the rule either, so that leaves the '17' card. If on the other side, we find the name of an alcoholic beverage then the rule is broken.

So why is this so much easier than the original task?

Enter evolutionary psychologist Leda Cosmides. As part of her PhD research she theorised that the alcohol task triggered an evolved cognitive mechanism designed to detect cheats or free riders. Recall from Chapter 3 that one of the huge problems with the evolution of cooperation is that cooperators are vulnerable to free riders who take the benefits of cooperation without paying the price. In order for cooperation to evolve, there needed to be a way of identifying and dealing with free riders and it is this that Cosmides believed was being triggered in the alcohol study. Some people are benefitting (drinking alcohol) without paying the price, or in this case meeting the criterion for drinking alcohol of being over the age of 18 (Cosmides and Tooby 1992).

There have been plenty of criticisms of Cosmides' approach (Buller 2005), but the approach demonstrates how useful evolutionary psychology can be in terms of making predictions. Theory predicts that cooperation cannot evolve without some way of being able to detect free riders – we *know* that cooperation has evolved so we *must* have evolved a free rider detection mechanism. And this may well be what Cosmides has found.

EVOLUTIONARY EXPLANATIONS OF STATISTICAL FALLACIES

In 2019 the casino and online gambling industry made 266 billion dollars, betting on sports such as horse racing made another 200 billion dollars and then there are the unregulated forms of gambling such as private games of poker. Gambling is big business, and it makes money *because* most people lose out most of the time. But why do people play if they are going to lose, that seems irrational?

One evolutionary answer is that life for our hunter–gatherer ancestors was a gamble. Sometimes a foraging expedition would be successful, at other times not, and gambling simply replicates this delicious uncertainty, and rewards with a shot of dopamine when success eventually happens. Another reason, it has been suggested (Gigerenzer, 1991), is that human brains are just not wired up to understand probability. The gamblers' fallacy is the belief that a run of bad luck will eventually be followed by a run of good: that losses will inevitably be followed by wins, and it is this belief that keeps punters at the roulette wheel or the blackjack table until their pockets have been emptied.

The gamblers' fallacy can easily be demonstrated: the following problem is adapted from one first presented to participants by (probably) Tversky and Kahneman.

Imagine you toss a coin five times and record each one. Which of the following represents the most likely outcome?

HHHHH

HTTHH

In their study (and still to this day) many people pick the bottom as being more likely, presumably because we know that a coin toss is a random event and the bottom one resembles our perception of randomness more than the top. But in fact, both are equally likely. The probability of a coin coming down either heads or tails is 1 in 2 or ½, and we can work out the probability of each of the above by multiplying ½ by itself for the number of throws. Because there are five throws in each that gives us (½)^5 or 1/32.

An alternative question is to imagine that we permit one more throw for each (giving six throws in total); which one is more likely, top or bottom, to be a heads? The answer, of course, it is the same or both as before. The coin cannot remember what has gone before so the likelihood of a head (or a tails) for both top and bottom is again ½, whatever your intuitions may be telling you.

The same applies to a roulette wheel, which is precisely so that the ball has an equal probability of landing in each of its slots. Just like tossing a coin, a roulette wheel has no memory, so if, for example on one spin the ball lands on zero, then the likelihood it lands on zero on the next spin is exactly the same.

So the gamblers' fallacy can't possibly be adaptive if it disagrees so starkly with probability theory, right? Well, no actually. The problem with coin tosses and roulette wheels is that they represent only part of probability theory, where the likelihood of one result is independent of the other and most of the world just isn't like that. In the real-world objects are not randomly distributed. Berries cluster on bushes, so if you find one berry there is a good chance that you will find another; many animals congregate into herds; water occurs in pools and so on. Even the weather is non-random, ultimately clumping into periods or relative predictability that we call 'seasons'. The point is that it is this clumpy world that we are adapted to and, when we go to the casino, we unconsciously make the assumption that it too will follow the same pattern. With sometimes disastrous results.

EVOLUTION AND MEMORY

As we all know, our memory sometimes lets us down. We turn up for an exam at the wrong time, forget an important phone number, or find that we have a very different recollection of an event as someone else.

Many evolutionists believe our memory was not designed to be a complete archive of all our experiences; it was designed to enable us to make good decisions, and to make them quickly (Gintis 2007). That sabre-tooth cat will not sit patiently while you try to recall whether or not it might eat you and therefore whether you should run away or not. An important memory process, therefore, is to take memories of raw experience (called **episodic memories**, Tulving 1972) and strip them of irrelevant detail and store only the essential elements to produce **semantic memories**, which can be accessed and acted on much more rapidly.

Another important process is our ability to forget. Storing too many memories could, again, slow down the process of retrieval, so memories that are deemed irrelevant are quietly erased. This is why you probably cannot remember what you had for breakfast two Fridays ago as such information is unlikely to be useful. This of course raises the question as to how we can determine in advance whether or not a memory is likely to be useful in the future. One factor is emotion. In times of great stress people will often have very detailed memories of the event, in extreme cases this can manifest itself as post-traumatic stress disorder (PTSD). Sufferers of PTSD can be overwhelmed by memories of traumatic events and can show hypervigilance in threatening situations. Although PTSD is clearly maladaptive, it may be an extreme form of a process that is evolutionarily useful. It would surely be good design to ensure that an animal that has had, for example, a near-death experience would learn from that experience and display vigilance in similar situations (Schacter 2001). Other research shows that non-human animals such as hares and elephants show a similar response to trauma as humans (Zanette et al. 2019).

A related phenomenon, which is known as **flashbulb memory** (Brown and Kulik, 1977) describes the phenomenon where people remember in great detail events surrounding emotionally important events, such as the assassination of President Kennedy, the death of Princess Diana, of 9–11 or, more recently, Donald Trump winning the US presidential elections. In all of these cases the emotion – of the individual themselves but also the people around them – are used to predict how consequential the event is and hence make it more likely to be stored in memory.

Finally recent evidence has suggested that our memory is adapted to our ancestral environment rather than our current one. For most of our evolutionary history, humans lived in hunter–gatherer communities on the African grasslands rather than in cities and towns and some claim that our memory is tuned to this ancestral environment (Nairne and Pandeirada 2008; Weinstein, Bugg and Roediger 2008). In a typical experiment, in one condition participants are given the following instructions.

> In this task we would like you to imagine that you are stranded in the grasslands of a foreign land, without any basic survival materials. Over the next few months, you'll need to find steady supplies of food and water and protect yourself from predators.

In another condition, they are given an almost identical instruction but the word 'grasslands' is replaced by 'city' and the word 'predators' by 'attackers'.

In both cases participants are given a list of 12 objects and asked how effective they thought each would be in protecting themselves. The objects don't seem to be particularly useful as they include things such as 'slipper', 'macaroni', 'tomb' and 'priest'. After rating these words participants are given a surprise recall task to see how many of the objects they can remember. In support of their hypothesis the researchers found that participants in the 'ancestral' condition recall more objects than those in the 'modern' condition despite the fact that the participants were city dwellers and had no direct experience of the African Savanah. The researchers explain this by suggesting that memory comes pre-wired to remember those things that are associated with ancestral survival.

SUMMARY

One of the benefits of evolutionary thinking is that it poses and tries to answer ultimate questions: what is the *purpose* of vision, reasoning and memory? As we have seen much of cognition seems to be orientated towards helping us to make good decisions that affect survival whether this be effectively navigating three-dimensional space, detecting cheats, foraging for food or making rapid assessments of threats and taking appropriate action. We have also seen in our discussion of memory that cognition and emotion often go hand in hand, and it is to this topic that we turn next.

EVOLUTION AND EMOTIONS

Trailblazing psychologist and philosopher William James is frequently described as the first person to consider the psychology of emotions. In his 1884 17-page article 'What is an emotion?', James considered the internal mechanisms behind human emotions. When it comes to emotions the real trailblazer was, however, Charles Darwin. In his book *The Expression of the Emotions in Man and Animals*, published some 12 years earlier than James' article, Darwin (1872) proposed that our emotional expressions were the products of natural and sexual selection and that they arose for communicative purposes. Based on careful observation (of humans and other species), experimentation and correspondence with experts from around the world, *The Expression of the Emotions* made five major contributions to our understanding of emotions (Ekman 2009):

1 Emotions are discrete, that is, for example, anger, fear, joy and disgust are distinct categories.
2 The human face has evolved to express emotions.

3 Human emotions are universal, that is, cross-culturally, we all show the same emotional expressions under the same circumstances (e.g. sadness when bereaved).
4 There is continuity in emotional expressions between us and other species (see Figure 5.3).
5 Specific emotional expressions are derived from the functions they served during our evolutionary past. An example of this is baring the teeth when in a rage as a preparation to attack.

Although psychologists frequently referred to James' early ideas on emotions, in contrast, during most of the twentieth century, Darwin's views were largely ignored (with one or two exceptions, Ekman 2009). This was largely due to the prevailing 'blank slate' social constructivist view that emotional expressions are learned and therefore culture specific (Armon-Jones 1985; Barrett 2018). Due, however, very much to the cross-cultural field work of Paul Ekman and his co-workers, since the 1970s, psychologists have become more favourable to Darwin's view of the adaptive significance of emotions (see Box 5.2).

Figure 5.3 Following Darwin, Ekman suggested there is continuity of emotional expression between humans and their relatives. Here two chimpanzees appear to share a smile

WHAT IS AN EMOTION?

Ironically, although James considered that he had answered this question back in 1884, psychologists today still debate the definition of what exactly an emotion is. In 2003 Robert Plutchick distilled all of the hundreds of proposed definitions down to 21 different ones. Fortunately, given we are concerned with evolutionary psychology, evolutionist Randolph Nesse has provided a definition that will serve our purpose well:

> Emotions are specialized states that adjust physiology, cognition, subjective experience, facial expressions, and behavior in ways that increase the ability to meet the adaptive challenges of situations that have recurred over the evolutionary history of a species.
>
> (Nesse 2019, p. 54)

Note that this definition is very much a functional evolutionary account since it makes it clear that emotions arose because they helped our ancestors to deal with recurrent adaptive challenges. It will be useful to bear this definition in mind when reading the remainder of this chapter.

BOX 5.2 DO WE HAVE UNIVERSAL EMOTIONAL EXPRESSIONS?

As we have seen, in his book of 1872, Darwin suggested cross-culturally humans share a number of discrete universal emotions. For many years this view was contested. During the 1970s, however, evidence began to accumulate which supported Darwin's view. This began in 1971 when Ekman and Friesen found people of the South Fore tribe from a remote area of Papua New Guinea correctly identified specific emotional facial expressions (such as disgust or rage) in photographs of Western individuals. Moreover, they were able to reproduce these expressions under similar circumstances. (Note, Ekman later went on to test recognition of emotional expressions in Chile, Argentina, Brazil, Japan and the United States, finding a very high level of cross-cultural agreement). Then in 1973 Eibl-Eibesfeldt showed that children born both blind and deaf produced the same emotional expressions under the same emotion-inducing circumstances as children who were able to see and hear. This suggests, that since these children would be unable to copy such expressions, they are largely innate. Eibl-Eibesfeldt also went on to demonstrate that individuals from various different countries use the same emotional expressions (such as the rapid surprised eyebrow raised expression when seeing a friend unexpectedly) over exactly the same time frame. Taken together, these observations provide evidence that 'basic emotions' (rage, fear, surprise, sadness, happiness, disgust and contempt according to Ekman) are the outcome of autonomous processes, which, in part, were inherited from our common ancestors. Note the 'in part' part of that last sentence is important. It is important that we don't see emotional expressions as pre-ordained and hard-wired with each having a specific brain circuit devoted to a single emotional state. Today many experts consider emotions as overlapping states that interact with each another, which, following commonly experienced situations, lead to the basic emotional expressions we observe cross-culturally (Barrett 2013; 2018). This is also true of Ekman who now perceives many emotions as families of related states (Ekman and Cordaro 2011).

CONTINUITY BETWEEN APES AND HUMANS IN EMOTIONAL EXPRESSIONS

The findings by Ekman and Friesen and those of Eibl-Eibesfeldt have helped to support Darwin's notion of universal facial expression (and underlying emotional experience) that evolved to aid communication of internal states in our Pleistocene ancestors. But what about the notion of continuity of emotional expressions between us and our simian relatives? For almost 100 years after Darwin first made this suggestion, it was largely ignored. Then in the 1960s a British ethologist provided evidence that he was also correct in this assumption. Richard Andrew (1963a; 1963b) documented how primate facial expressions are a secondary consequence of the vocalisations they produce when emotionally aroused. For example, the shriek that many monkeys make when in fear involves pulling the lips back into a 'fear-grin'. This fear grin is common across primate species and is also observed in humans. Andrew suggested that, having originally evolved to allow

Figure 5.4 The 59-year-old chimpanzee Cheetah (of Tarzan film fame) shares a common friendly grin with his human companion during a painting session

the appropriate sound to be made, the facial gesture then evolved into a silent grin that we see today. Hence, with the fear grin and other common expressions that were used under similar circumstances, Andrew was able to demonstrate continuity of expression between humans and other primates. In support of Andrew, primatologist Frans de Waal has suggested primate facial expressions observed during play and during submission can be mapped onto the expressions humans use when laughing and smiling respectively (de Waal 2003). Figure 5.4 shows a typical chimpanzee expression.

NEUROLOGICAL BASES OF EMOTIONS

Over recent years the field of neuroscience has been developed in order to provide a better understanding of underlying neural correlates of internal states and behaviour. In particular, **cognitive neuroscience**, as we have seen, developed during the 1980s and this was followed in the 1990s by the development of **affective neuroscience** (Passingham 2016). Affective, in this context, refers to mood, personality and emotions. Hence affective neuroscience is concerned with the neurological bases of emotional states. One of the main tools of neuroscience today is the use of imaging techniques such as fMRI. Another is **deep brain stimulation** (DBS) whereby researchers stimulate areas within the brain and then observe a human or animal's response. The neuropsychologist, who coined the term affective neuroscience, Jaak Panksepp, has made use of DBS to uncover evidence supporting Darwin's notion of continuity between humans and other species in their emotional states. In Panksepp's model, humans share with other mammalian species seven neurological circuits that are associated with different forms of emotional arousal including four that are rewarding (seeking, lust, care and play) and three that are punishing (rage, fear and panic). These are outlined in Table 5.1. It should be noted that in Panksepp's model these circuits are not genetically determined but genetically influenced and require environmental feedback to form properly.

Table 5.1 Jaak Panksepp's proposed seven core emotional systems

Core emotional system	*Evoked by and function of system*
Anger/Rage	Evoked by competition for resources. Most frequently aroused by frustration.
Fear	Evoked by danger. Two pathways – fast one which helps rapid action and slower one which is more considered.
Sexual lust	Evoked by presence of appropriate attractive other. Develops during puberty.
Care system	Evoked when nurturance (generally of young) is appropriate. For humans, occurs in both females and males.
Separation distress	Evoked in young when away from parent (usually mother). Can lead to crying and, in extreme cases, panic.
Play system	Evoked in young by presence of other individuals or appropriate objects. Include feelings of joy and expressed by laughing.
Seeking system	Motivated by desire to seek novelty and often related to obtaining resources and is connected to appraisal of the environment.

It is worth noting that these overlap with, but are not identical to, Ekman's seven **basic emotions** (Panksepp 1998; Panksepp and Davis 2018). But of course, Ekman is largely concerned with emotional facial expression, whereas Panksepp is concerned with neurological circuits underpinning emotional experience. So, we should not expect a perfect mapping of one on to the other. To Panksepp, sharing similar underlying neural hardware to support emotional states makes sense because all organisms with complex nervous systems, such as vertebrates, face broadly similar emotion-inducing challenges and therefore, would benefit from making use of broadly similar neuronal circuitry.

Imaging techniques have also uncovered specific areas of the brain that are associated with emotional processing and response. Two areas in particular are the **amygdala** and the **orbitofrontal cortex**. It is worth considering each briefly. The amygdala (which, due to its shape, is Latin for 'almond') receives a great deal of sensory information and information concerning memory and attention from other brain areas. It also has connections with the frontal lobes, which are involved in planning and decision making. This means that the amygdala sits between sensory information coming in and attentional, memory and emotional responses going out. Imagining studies show the amygdala to be particularly active when we experience fear. Furthermore, electrical stimulation of the amygdala leads to fear responses and individuals who have had damage to this part of the brain have odd or no fear response (Ray 2013). In fact, one woman who is always referred to as 'SM', having suffered damage to the amygdala, was no longer able to experience fear. Interestingly, she was able to experience other emotions such as happiness and anger. SM was able to withstand things that would previously have caused her a great deal of fear such as the presence of spiders and snakes and entering a 'haunted house'. The involvement of the amygdala in fear processing appears to be as true for other mammalian species as it is for our own (LeDoux 2012).

The orbitofrontal cortex (OFC) is so named because it is the portion of the cortex (the brain's outer 'rind') of the prefrontal lobes that is found just above the orbit of the eyes. Intriguingly, studies demonstrate that the right OFC is involved in negative affect whereas the left is associated with positive affect (an example of lateralisation, Ray 2013). While, like the amygdala, the OFC is associated with emotional processing, damage here leads to more complex changes. People who have damage to the OFC do not appear to be aware of the consequences of their actions, often leading to embarrassing behaviour. Some experts consider the OFC to be involved in our capacity to generate an emotional state within ourselves through cognition and, at times, to override emotional responses (Ray 2013). That is, by thinking about a situation (current, past or future) we can induce or reduce our emotional state. Of course, talking therapy and mindfulness would be doomed to failure without this ability. This means that, while there is clear evidence of continuity between ourselves and other primates with regard to emotional expressions (and arguably emotional experience), there are areas where our superior cognitive abilities allow us to use our emotions in more refined ways. We can, for example, analyse our initial emotional responses and hence transform them. We can also experience emotional responses to objects of art and music. To play 'devil's advocate', it is entirely possible, however, that other species such as avians can have an emotional experience when hearing, for example, another bird's song or in the case of peahens when seeing a particularly fine peacock's tail.

We have outlined two important brain regions, which along with others, help to process and moderate our emotions. Of course, neither of these operates in isolation and indeed some experts today consider that the OFC (and other parts of the cortex of the brain), as more recently evolved entities, can maintain a controlling influence over deeper more ancient parts of the brain (such as the amygdala) (Sapolsky 2018).

FUNCTIONAL EXPLANATIONS OF EMOTIONAL STATES

Although Darwin was the first to propose emotional expressions were the products of evolution, his emphasis on their communicative purpose meant that he did not really consider the adaptive function of each emotional experience. At the turn of the last century, however, emotions expert Paul Ekman suggested they evolved in order to allow us to deal with what he calls ancient recurrent **fundamental life tasks** (Ekman 1999). Fundamental life tasks are universal human challenges such as frustrations, losses and accomplishments. More specifically, our ancestors had to, for example, escape predators and hostile strangers, fall in love and decide when to hold their ground at times when challenged. This suggests that, when faced with a fundamental life task, those better able to respond with the appropriate emotions would be more likely to survive and pass on their genes for such responses. If this is the case, then we may be able to propose functions for specific emotional states, both positive and negative.

FUNCTIONS OF NEGATIVE EMOTIONAL STATES

While negative emotions are, by definition, unpleasant, it is vital that we have these within our emotional repertoire. Negative emotions motivate us to change our ways, either immediately (such as when threatened) or in the longer term (look after loved ones more carefully).

Ekman (1999), as we have seen, has suggested that negative emotions help us to achieve fundamental life tasks. Fear, for example, can include panic and agoraphobia, leading to enhanced vigilance and flight responses. Note these are different manifestations of fear, suggesting this emotion can take different forms, each of which might be applied to a different fundamental life task. Likewise, anger, which is generally a response to others, can often take the form of moral or righteous indignation. In such cases it is generally related to detecting and acting on free riders. Such a state of anger may function to make it explicit to the free rider that their lack of reciprocation has been spotted and that, unless they change their ways, they are likely to be ostracised. This form of anger is generally felt as a 'simmering' state. Rage, however, is more of an act of anger that prepares someone to fight back immediately when physically or verbally attacked. Another negative emotional state is sadness. According to Ekman, the withdrawal from normal activities that we see when people are sad signals to others that they require aid and support. Finally, disgust makes us withdraw from noxious stimuli (both physical and psychological, such as when someone has behaved very badly to others). Disgust responses signal to others they need to avoid this stimulus and hence is generally a social signal.

Overall, both the expression and experience of negative emotions serve to narrow attention. That is, we become far less likely to be distracted by other stimuli when in a negative emotional state. Negative emotions also produce physiological and behavioural changes, which, no doubt, would have increased survival in the ancestral environment and simultaneously communicate to others our change in internal state.

BOX 5.3 DO BASIC EMOTIONS REALLY SERVE SPECIFIC FUNCTIONS?

Although many evolutionists share the belief in the concept of humans having a number of universal basic emotions serving quite specific functions, some experts today consider this is a simplification of the real story. Recently, Randolph Nesse has modified his view on this question. While he still considers emotional states evolved to solve ancient adaptive problems, rather than specifying functions for basic emotions, he now views them as 'as special modes of operation that increase ability to cope with certain situations' (Nesse 2019 p. 53). This nuanced view suggests that, while humans share emotional states cross-culturally, a basic emotion can have more than one defined function. Furthermore, in order to understand basic emotional responses, we always need to reflect on the situational context. For example, when threatened or bereaved, becoming happy is totally impractical, whereas demonstrating anxiety and sadness are appropriate responses respectively. We should also bear in mind that it is possible to feel happiness at achieving success and at seeing an enemy's efforts completely nose-dive. Not all positive emotions are honourable!

FUNCTIONS OF POSITIVE EMOTIONAL STATES

In some respects, it is easier to foresee negative emotional states as serving a purpose than positive ones. At first sight it appears difficult to imagine how on earth being happy might be adaptive? When, however, we focus in on the things that make us happy then it soon becomes apparent it is precisely the sort of activities and experiences that make us happy which would most likely have helped our ancestors to boost their inclusive fitness (that is pass on copies of their genes). Think of things that make most people happy. Smiling babies, sweet food, sex with a loving partner are just some of the things that no doubt our ancestors found equally rewarding and hence, since we all seek happiness, can be considered adaptive (von Hippel 2018). One expert who has made a study of positive emotions such as happiness is Barbara Fredrickson. Fredrickson has turned the notion of negative emotions serving to narrow focus on its head by developing a theory that positive emotions do just the opposite in as much as they serve to broaden it. She calls this the 'broaden-and-build' theory of positive emotions (Fredrickson 1998; 2013). Fredrickson's broaden-and-build theory proposes positive emotions evolved to help expand social networks, build personal resources and enrich our knowledge base. Fredrickson has focused her attention on joy, contentment, interest and love.

In the case of joy, this playful emotion helps us to find out about peers in a non-threatening way. Joy is also experienced in a romantic relationship, as lovers enjoy each other's company (while also finding out more about them, such as how committed to the relationship they might be). Such joy has clear implications for reproductive success (even though the loving couple might not perceive it in quite that way!). Contentment that follows childbirth helps to shift parental priorities to the new-born. Interest causes exploration, which thereby increases our knowledge base. This, in turn, can increase our problem-solving skills, arguably enhancing the chances of survival. Contentment involves savouring our accomplishments, which, in turn, may increase the chance of repeating fruitful strategies. Love, in all its forms, be it romantic, motherly/fatherly, brotherly/sisterly or companionate, clearly had selective advantages for our ancestors. We can see it as a frequent component, both in reciprocal altruism and as a part of the kin selected altruism in our own species (see Chapter 3).

Recently Fredrickson and her co-researcher Thomas Joiner have developed the concept of the **broaden-and-build** theory of positive emotions into what has become known as the **upward spiral theory** of lifestyle change. Here, positive emotions are utilised to improve a person's future health-related behaviours (illustrated in Figure 5.5, based on Fredrickson and Joiner 2018).

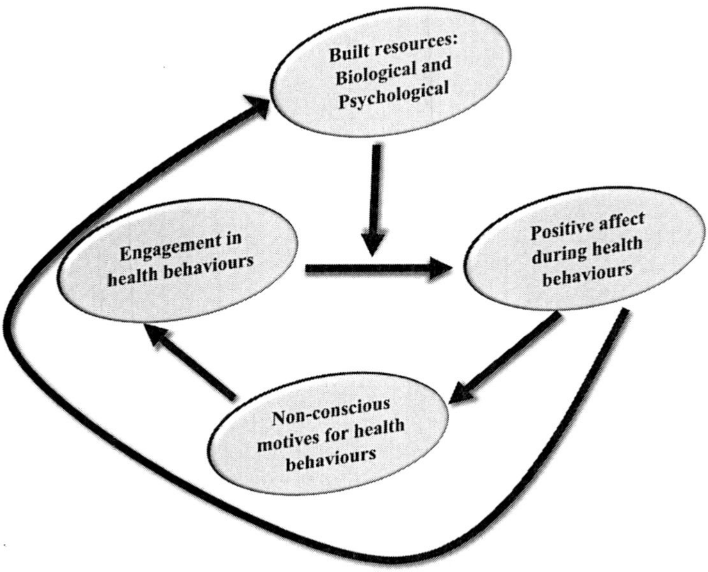

Figure 5.5 Upward spiral model of lifestyle change (Redrawn based on Fredrickson and Joiner 2018)

The upward spiral theory of lifestyle change model has an inner and an outer loop. Considering the inner loop, when individuals have positive emotional experiences in health-related behaviours, they then develop non-conscious motives for further positive health-related behaviours. The outer loop then demonstrates how such behaviours and internal states become supported by developing psychological and biological resources. An example of a biological resource might be reduced resting blood pressure and pulse rate, while a psychological resource might be developing positivity of purpose in life. In this model, the outer loop feeds into and supports the inner loop. According to Fredrickson and Joiner, the ability to enter into an upward spiral is a specific human adaptation allowing for recovery from an enduring negative emotional state.

This development of an upward spiral of lifestyle change has been influential and illustrates how research work based within an evolutionary framework can be more than esoteric in nature.

People suffering from low self-esteem and negative health-related practices can help to improve both their mental and physical health by applying this model of lifestyle change.

Today, while there may be debates about the specific functions of emotional states, due to the work of experts such as Ekman, Nesse and Frederickson, it would be difficult to argue that our evolutionary heritage has played no part in the internal feelings we all experience.

SUMMARY

The cognitive approach has proved to be very effective in helping psychologists to understand the mechanisms and processes involved in thinking and doing. One of its limitations is that it tends to provide a picture of human cognition that is quite piecemeal. Like the story of the blind men encountering an elephant, each person perceives the animal in different ways. The man feeling the tusk sees the elephant as being like a spear, the one touching the trunk as a snake, the one touching the ears as a fan and so on. In order to see the elephant as it truly is we need to put all of these elements together. The study of cognition is similarly atomistic; cognitive psychologists study vision, reasoning, memory and many other topics but these are seldom put together to see how they interact and give a more complete picture of the whole person. By considering cognition from an ultimate perspective based on evolutionary function, we will be in a better place to do this. As we have seen above, one unifying theme is that cognition functions to make rapid and sensible decisions regarding fitness. Moreover, an even more complete picture of human thought needs to consider the importance of emotion in decision making.

In 1872 Darwin first suggested that emotional expressions arose due to their adaptive value in communication. He also proposed emotional expressions show similarities between humans and other species and are virtually identical across human cultures. During the latter years of the twentieth century, when considering 'basic emotions' (happiness, sadness, disgust, rage, fear, surprise and contempt), Paul Ekman found strong evidence that people from widely differing cultures both recognise and make use of the same expressions. Richard Andrew found evidence that primates make use of similar facial expression to humans and do so under broadly similar social circumstances. Through use of 'deep brain stimulation' Jaak Panksepp suggested we and other species have seven core neurological emotional systems, which are evoked by broadly similar stimuli (such as danger and competition) and which serve the same underlying functions. Activation of the amygdala is associated with fear responses, while the orbitofrontal cortex is associated with processing of emotional processes including activation and inhibition of socially appropriate responses. Functions have been proposed for negative emotions such as fear serving to aid flight response and anger being used to respond to free riders. Barbara Fredrickson has also proposed functional explanations for positive emotions as a part of her 'broaden and build theory'. Joy, for example, helps us to enjoy each other's company and contentment helps us to appraise our circumstances and shift priorities.

FURTHER READING

von Hippel, W. (2018) *The Social Leap: The New Evolutionary Science of Who We Are, Where We Came From, and What Makes Us Happy*. New York: HarperCollins.

Sapolsky, R. M. (2018) *Behave: The Biology of Humans at Our Best and Worst*. New York: Penguin.

Taylor, S. and Workman, L. (2021) *Cognitive Psychology: The Basics*. London: Routledge.

6

WHY DO PEOPLE VARY? INDIVIDUAL DIFFERENCES AND MENTAL ILLNESS

INDIVIDUAL DIFFERENCES: WHY AREN'T WE ALL THE SAME?

Contrary to the belief of many social scientists, evolutionary psychologists are firmly of the view that there is a phenomenon that we can label 'human nature'. As we saw in Chapter 5, there is clear evidence that there are intrinsic, essential qualities such as cognitive and emotional processes that we, as a species, all share. There is, however, an important branch of psychology for which this view might seem problematic – the field of individual differences. This field, which is also known as **differential psychology**, considers both how and why people vary in terms of personality and intelligence. The problem here is that, if there is a universal human nature, then why do we all appear to differ so much? We regularly describe people as extravert or shy, bold or fearful and even bright or dull (if perhaps not to their faces). During most of the early development of evolutionary approaches to human behaviour, this potentially embarrassing fact was largely ignored as evolutionary psychologists showed little interest in individual differences, preferring instead to concentrate on topics such as cheater detection, mating preferences and foraging mechanisms. Over the last 15 years or so, however, some evolutionary psychologists have begun to explore ways in which individual differences can be integrated into accounts of an evolved human nature (Nettle 2006; Buss and Hawley 2011; Furnham and Kanazawa 2020). Concentrating mainly on personality, in this chapter we consider the

DOI: 10.4324/9780429274428-6

theories that have been developed to explain, within an evolutionary framework, why it is that humans vary in the ways they do. We then move on to examine why it is that some people vary so much from what we normally expect, that they are considered to have serious mental health issues. We begin with an exploration of how we might divide up the various aspects of personality.

THE STRUCTURE OF PERSONALITY

Differential psychologists have long argued over how many dimensions or factors personality might be distilled down to. Hans Eysenck was of the view that we share only three basic personality factors – extraversion, neuroticism and psychoticism (Eysenck and Eysenck 1976). In contrast, Raymond Cattell (1965) proposed 16, including warmth, reasoning and sensitivity. We can think of these two psychologists as representing extreme 'clumpers' and 'splitters'. That is, some perceive there to be very few dimensions to personality while others hold the view that there are many. Fortunately for us, we don't have to review the various debates proposed by each camp, as, since the late 1980s, personality psychologists have converged on a middle ground **five factor model** (McCrae and Costa 1987). In McCrae and Costa's model the 'big five' dimensions are:

Openness to experience--------------------	Closed-minded
(Adventurous)	(Conservative)
Conscientious----------------------------	Unconscientious
(Self-disciplined)	(Impulsive)
Extraversion-----------------------------	Introversion
(Outgoing)	(Reserved)
Agreeableness----------------------------	Disagreeableness
(Nice)	(Unpleasant)
Neuroticism------------------------------	Stability
(Anxious)	(Calm)

(Note that by taking the first letter of each factor/dimension on the left we can create a useful mnemonic by spelling out the word 'OCEAN'.)

The reason there is broad consensus on the five factor model is because tests show that they stand up to scrutiny cross-culturally and because, knowing a score on one dimension does not predict how well a person scores on any of the other four (suggesting they really are independent (Furnham and Kanazawa 2020)). You may be thinking at this point, what exactly does it mean to say that personality can be described by five dimensions? What this means is that, by completing a personality questionnaire (sometimes called an 'inventory'), psychologists can take your answers and produce a

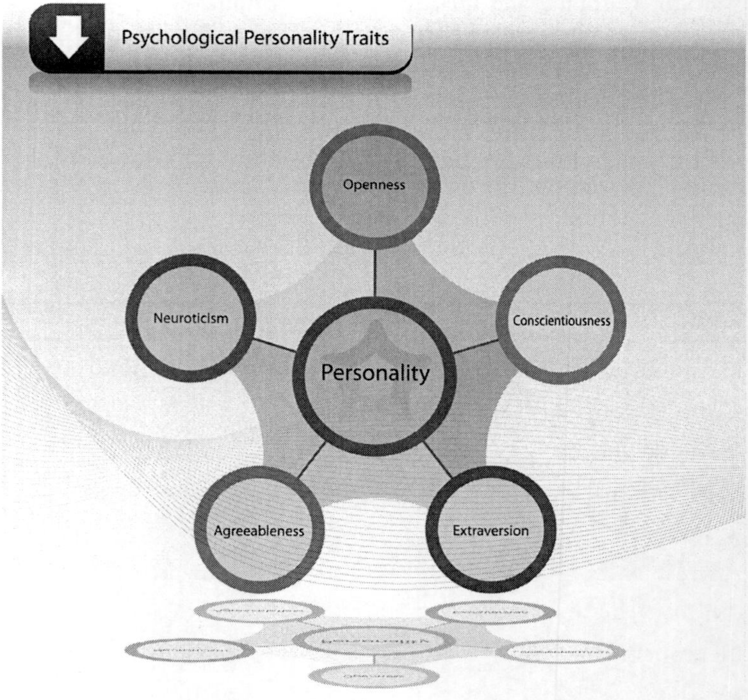

Figure 6.1 The structure of personality traits according to the five factor model

score (e.g. 1–10) showing how you compare with the rest of the population on each of the five. Your score on each of the big five can be considered as your 'personality profile'. Here are some examples of the types of questions you might encounter if you fill in one of these questionnaires:

- I enjoy meeting people with new ideas (openness)
- I think of other's feelings before acting (agreeableness)
- I always complete projects (conscientiousness)
- I am often the life and soul of a party (extraversion)
- I find I am more anxious than most other people (neuroticism).

BOX 6.1 EVOLUTION AND INTELLIGENCE: WHY THE VARIABILITY?

Some differential psychologists focus on intelligence rather than personality. While there are debates as to how we should define intelligence, most psychologists agree that it involves reasoning, planning and, importantly, problem-solving. Since the advent of evolutionary psychology, some psychologists have considered how intellectual abilities might have been adapted to the ancestral past. One in particular, Howard Gardner, has suggested that we should expand traditional views of intelligence to factor in survival abilities. This means that, in addition to linguistic and mathematical ability, we should broaden intelligence to include, for example, the ability to read the emotions of others and of ourselves. Gardner's expanded view of intelligence includes eight different human abilities (Gardner 2006; 2010):

1 Linguistic (language use)
2 Logical-mathematical (mathematical reasoning)
3 Visuospatial (ability to mentally manipulate objects in space)
4 Musical (perception of and production of music)
5 Bodily-kinesthetic (control body movements)
6 Interpersonal (understanding others)
7 Intrapersonal (understand oneself)
8 Naturalistic (understanding and reading the natural world).

Note that only the first three are normally measured in a traditional IQ test. Yet, when it comes to survival and reproduction, the remaining five would clearly be of advantage to our ancestors. They may also be of advantage in life today, albeit less easily measured than the first three (Sternberg 2021).

EVOLUTION AND PERSONALITY

Given the level of variability we see between people, some might argue that personality is free from evolutionary processes and subject instead to random societal and cultural whims? There are two problems with this view. The first problem is the fact that each of the big five factors has a high degree of heritability (ranging from 0.35 to 0.5, Plomin et al. 2012; Plomin 2018). This suggests almost half of the variation between people in these personality factors can be accounted for by genetic differences between them. If genes are involved in the development of personality, then this suggests evolutionary factors have also been at work. The second problem is there is little evidence that any of the big five are substantially influenced by culture (Furnham and Cheg 2015; Furnham and Kanazawa 2020). Hence, knowing which culture someone is raised in does not allow you to predict their personality, suggesting the importance of biological variables in the development of the big five.

These findings raise two rather large questions. First, what advantages (in terms of solving ancestral challenges) might having variability in the big five have? And second, how do evolutionists account for this variability? With regard to the first question, Daniel Nettle has suggested there are costs and benefits to each of the big five factors. With regard to the second question, evolutionary psychologists have proposed a range of explanations for the variability we observe today. We consider four of these in the next section. But with regard to the first question, the proposed benefits (and costs) for each of the big five are considered in Table 6.1.

Considering Table 6.1, we should point out that, just as there is more than one way to skin the proverbial cat, different

Table 6.1 Benefits and costs (in evolutionary terms) to each of the big five personality factors

Big five personality dimensions	*Positive aspects of factor*	*Negative aspects of factor*
Openness to Closedness	People who score high on openness are curious and creative. These factors often make them attractive to others. People who are high on closedness do not like to try untested ways.	Those who score highly on openness can also have unusual beliefs leading to them being considered 'mad' by some others. Those high on closedness can miss out on new opportunities.
Conscientiousness to Unconscientiousness	Conscientious people show order and perseverance. They 'pitch in' and plan for future events. Unconscientious people can easily shift their priorities in times of change.	Conscientious individuals are often slow to adapt to change. Unconscientious individuals rarely complete tasks and let others down regularly.
Extraversion to Introversion	Being highly social and sensation seeking, extraverts have more sexual partners leading to greater mating success. Introverts are a 'safer bet' in that they are more likely to stay faithful. This makes for more reliable parenting skills.	Extraverts are more prone to infidelity and relationship breakup, exposing offspring to stepparents who might invest less in them. Introverts have fewer sexual partners than extraverts, meaning, arguably, they are likely to leave fewer offspring.
Agreeableness to Disagreeableness	Being kind and empathic, individuals who score highly on agreeableness, make for good romantic partners. Those low on agreeableness can be successful by exploiting others.	Highly agreeable people can be too trusting and pay more attention to the needs of others. Highly disagreeable individuals can be ostracised when others spot this trait.
Neuroticism to Stability	Neurotic people may request and receive a great deal of support from others. Highly stable people are respected and make for good long-term partners.	Highly neurotic people may eventually be rejected due to their 'neediness' and low mood. It is difficult to perceive negative aspects as being highly stable bar the fact that they are less likely to request support.

Source: Based largely on Nettle 2006 and Furnham and Kanazawa 2020.

combinations of scores on each of the big five can lead to success (in terms of surviving and passing on your genes). For example, being high on agreeableness but low on extraversion can lead to high achievement. Likewise, being high on neuroticism but again high on agreeableness means that others are more likely to help you out. This, of course, is also true of combinations that we might think of as successful on their own but, when combined, lead to problems. An example of this is those who score highly both on conscientiousness and on agreeableness. This might sound like an ideal combination. Unfortunately, such people are often considered to be 'too nice for their own good' and are more likely to be exploited by others (particularly by those low on both dimensions). The take home point here is we need to look at all five in combination and that what is perceived as a 'poor score' on one, when combined with a 'good score' on another, might have actually led to a successful strategy when considering inclusive fitness in the ancestral past. Each, of course, will be environmentally contingent.

EVOLUTIONARY EXPLANATIONS FOR INDIVIDUAL DIFFERENCES

While Table 6.1 helps us to understand how scoring both high and low on each of the big five can, under the right circumstances, aid inclusive fitness, it still does not really explain how such variability comes about? Why, during the EEA, did we not simply evolve one successful combination of these factors that we all share? In order to seek an answer to this question, in recent years, evolutionists have developed a number of explanations. Here we consider four of the most influential ones.

FREQUENCY DEPENDENT SELECTION

One rather simplistic view of evolution is that there exist optimum settings for all traits. This suggests, there is such a thing as a perfect set of adaptations for each species. The problem with this way of thinking is that, what works well for you, may largely depend on what everybody else is doing. For example, if everybody else acts with a reasonable degree of altruism then it may pay you (in evolutionary terms) to be somewhat more selfish (see Chapter 1). In fact, it has even been proposed that, because most of us are reasonably altruistic, then the benefits of exploitation lead to the selection of psychopathic behaviour in a minority of the population (Mealey 1995). This, of course only works if the proportion of exploitive psychopaths is relatively low (once a large proportion act in this way then the whole reciprocal altruism system breaks down). This scenario of altruists to non-altruists illustrates a phenomenon known as **frequency dependent selection**. That is, if everybody else is following one strategy then, provided you are in the minority, it may well pay you to adopt a rarer strategy. Today it is well established that, in the animal kingdom, frequency-dependent selection is a potent force maintaining variation in populations (Wolf and McNamara 2012). Examples of this include the number of 'bold' and 'timid' birds in a population and differing levels of aggression in all manner of species (Dingemanse et al. 2004; Duckworth 2010). Returning to humans, rather like the example of psychopathic individuals, but to a lessor extreme, we can easily imagine how in a population that is chock-a-block full of highly conscientious individuals or of those who score highly on openness, it may pay you to have offspring who adopt a range of different strategies. Hence, as in other species, frequency-dependent selection is likely to be a potent selective force, maintaining variability in personality dimensions within our species.

SEX AND RANDOM VARIATION AROUND THE MEAN

Sexually reproducing organisms randomly discard half of their genes each time they reproduce (see Chapter 1). These are then combined with the genes of another (who likewise has randomly discarded 50 per cent of their genes). This means that successful gene combinations are broken up and recombined every time a new individual is created. The randomness of this process sets limits on what natural and sexual selection can achieve and introduces unavoidable 'noise' into the system. Hence, when considering a population, many of our traits form a **normal distribution** (a 'bell shaped curve') around the mean. Think of the height of women you know. The majority will be between five feet and five feet nine. As we move away from this central tendency, increasingly smaller proportions of the population will be observed (such as women who are four feet four or six feet four). We can also think of this when considering personality. You probably could estimate where all of your friends might fall on each of the big five dimensions. There will no doubt be a fair degree of variation here, but we suspect none of them will be so extraverted that you can't bear to be in the same room as them, or so introverted that they never, ever join in discussion (both extremes do not necessarily make for good company). Moreover, the larger the number of genes involved in the development of a trait, the greater the opportunity for variation in said trait. Today we know that personality factors are all very polygenic (their development involves a large number of genes, see Chapter 1 and Plomin 2018). Hence, sexual reproduction, and the polygenic nature of many personality traits leads to a degree of variation in our (and no doubt other) species.

Before considering our next reason for variability, we need to add one proviso. That is, when it comes to variation in personality between people, we all have a tendency to exaggerate differences. Yes, some people are far more agreeable than others, some are far more open to new ideas. Compared to say chimpanzees, however, we are, as a species highly agreeable and highly open to new ideas (very rare exceptions are, for example, psychopaths). Place 200 unfamiliar chimps on an airplane for a long-haul flight and they would rip each other apart. Humans are actually really quite similar to each other in that the vast majority of us favour cooperation over conflict. The differences we perceive are tiny compared to the similarities. It no doubt paid our ancestors to be able to distinguish quite small differences between people in order to avoid, for example, free riders.

REACTIVE HERITABILITY

The **reactive heritability hypothesis** demonstrates how nature and nurture interact in the development of personality. The idea here is that, as we grow up, we receive feedback from others about many of our genetically influenced traits. Of particular importance is our physical appearance. How people treat us based on our physical attributes then has a knock-on effect on the development of our personality traits. In the case of, for example, a particularly pretty, young girl, people are more likely to pay attention to her and she then comes to realise that others are likely to be benevolent to her when she smiles and acts in a friendly way. This means that she later scores highly on agreeableness and on extraversion since she is unlikely to be shy of other people. Similarly, a well-built boy might learn via feedback from others that children are likely to be submissive to him. This, in turn, can lead to confidence and being used to others allowing him to hold forth. This, of course sounds quite speculative. There is, however, empirical evidence that attractive females and physically robust males both score more highly on extraversion than those who are less attractive or well built (Lukaszewski and Roney 2011; Lukaszewski and von Rueden 2015). Hence, receiving feedback from others then influences the development of personality traits and helps to explain why we all differ to the degree that we do. Behavioural geneticists and evolutionary psychologists call this an 'evocative relationship' between genes and environment (Workman and Reader 2021).

BOX 6.2 THE NURTURE ASSUMPTION: DOES PARENTAL SOCIALISATION MAKE A DIFFERENCE?

We often assume that how we bring our children up has an enormous impact on the way they turn out. But does this commonly held nurture assumption stand up to scrutiny? In 1998 developmentalist Judith Rich Harris published a book that suggested how we treat our children has virtually no influence on the personalities they eventually develop. In her controversial book *The Nurture Assumption: Why Children Turn Out the Way They Do*, Harris (1998; 2009) argued persuasively that how parents raise their children has little effect on them because they are socialised largely by their peers. She calls this **group socialisation theory**. People who have not studied the evidence tend to find this notion absurd. People who have studied the evidence are often astonished at how weak the evidence for the nurture assumption is. The best way to understand Harris' argument is to read her very accessible book. But, in brief, one of the strongest forms of supportive evidence comes from the work of behavioural geneticists who study sources of variation in people. Behavioural geneticists split variation in personality into three areas: heritability (genes), shared environment (shared experiences in the family) and the non-shared environment (non-shared experiences that come mainly from outside of the family). Through a large number of studies, they have established the general rule of thumb that adult personality follows a 50–0–50 pattern. That is, 50 per cent of variability is heritable, 0 per cent is due to shared home environment and 50 per cent is due to the non-shared (largely outside the home) environment. This raises the question, why did developmental psychologists consider parental socialisation to be so important in the development of a child's personality? As Harris points out, many studies find positive correlations between parents and offspring in features such as how aggressive they are. Developmentalists then assume that the child is modelling on the parent. However, as Harris points out, such studies ignore the effects of shared genes between parent and offspring. Moreover, they also ignore child-to-parent effects. In other words, having a child that shows signs of aggression leads, in turn, to aggressive responses in the adults in their interactions with the child. This, of course, also works for all aspects of personality as we tend to respond in kind to the way others (including our children) treat us. Some critics have taken issue with the notion that how we treat children has no effect on them. Harris counters this by pointing out that she considers parents to be of utmost importance since they provide the child with all of their genes and they have a major influence on who they mix with (Harris and Workman 2016).

BIRTH ORDER EFFECTS

How similar are you to your brothers and sisters? Perhaps a more pertinent question is – how different from them are you? It's often observed that siblings are like 'chalk and cheese' and, in fact, appear to differ from each other to a greater extent than they do, say to their friends. If this is the case, then, given full siblings share 50 per cent of the genes by common descent, we might ask where does this variation come from? Anecdotally, there is a widespread belief that birth order affects the way children behave. First-borns are seen as mature and last-borns as spoilt (especially if they appear some years after the previous child). The question is, are these just urban myths, like the notion that chewing gum stays in your stomach for seven years or that chocolate gives you acne, or do they actually stand up to scrutiny? Some psychologists have suggested, not only do they stand up to scrutiny, but that birth order effects on personality are adaptations, rather than epiphenomena of family life.

The first psychologist to suggest that birth order might have a serious impact on personality was the late nineteenth- and early twentieth-century Austrian psychotherapist Alfred Adler. Adler (1928) argued that first-borns were more dutiful and conservative, but also more prone to neuroticism since they experienced 'dethronement' when the second child came along. As an influential figure in the development of twentieth-century psychology, Alder's views were often accepted in books and magazine articles during the last century. It was, however, based on personal family experience and highly speculative. Then in the 1950s Helen Koch published two empirical studies involving large samples that demonstrated significant differences between siblings related to birth order. Koch found, relative to later-borns, first-borns were more self-confident, competitive and emotionally intense (Koch 1955, 1956). Note these observations are quite close to those suggested by Adler. A number of psychologists followed up Koch's work in the second half of the twentieth century, but it was only in 1996 that Harvard psychologist Frank Sulloway proposed an evolutionary explanation for this family variability. In his book *Born to Rebel*, Sulloway suggested siblings differ from each other because having variability in the family allows the unit to exploit a wider variety of resources (Sulloway 1996). Having, for example, offspring who are, in turn, conscientious, bold, agreeable and highly open to new ideas is a superior strategy to having children who are identical in these traits. Not only does this help exploitation of the environment (including the social environment) but it also means that children do not find themselves in regular competition for family roles. How, we might ask, does this variability arise? According to Sulloway, due to their positions in terms of birth order, different family members gravitate towards different 'ecological niches'. First-borns, for example, tend to be more competitive and dominating. Later-borns, however, score higher on agreeableness, possibly because they are less competitive. First-borns, of course, are physically and cognitively more advanced than their siblings, which means they become used to dominating later-borns to get their way. Later-borns, in contrast, tend to develop more cooperative ways because this was more successful for them during childhood; hence a higher level of agreeableness. For their part, despite being lower in agreeableness, first-borns are on average higher in conscientiousness, due perhaps to having, at times, to play the role of surrogate parent to their younger siblings (Sulloway 2020).

Although Sulloway's findings are statistically significant we should note they have relatively small overall effects. It may be that birth order effects, while notable, are of less importance than the other three sources of variability presented above. What is interesting about birth order effects is that the variability emerges due largely to non-genetic factors.

EVOLUTION AND MENTAL HEALTH

So far, we have considered why it is that people vary from an evolutionary perspective. Some people vary quite considerably from society's expectations both in their behaviour and in relation to their internal state. Some may appear to have inappropriately extreme emotional states (such as depression or severe anxiety), others may report they hear voices that only they perceive. In such cases people are generally considered to have mental health issues. In fact, in the West today around one in four people will experience some form of a mental health issue. While there are many forms of mental illness, most of these can be divided into affective disorders (anxiety and depression) and psychotic disorders (including **schizophrenia**, see later). If we can make use of evolutionary psychology to help explain variability in personality, then, arguably we should also be able to make use of the ultimate perspective to explore the disturbingly high rate of vulnerability? Over the last 30 years a relatively small number of specialists have attempted to answer this question and, in doing so, have developed a new subfield of evolutionary psychology known by various names such as evolutionary medicine, **Darwinian medicine**, evolutionary psychiatry and evolutionary psychopathology (Abed and St John-Smith 2022). It is worth noting that the first two terms have a slightly different meaning to the latter two; evolutionary medicine and Darwinian medicine consider all health-related problems, whereas evolutionary psychiatry and evolutionary psychopathology are more specialised in that they are restricted to mental health issues. One of the founders of evolutionary medicine is the Arizona State University evolutionary psychiatrist Randolph Nesse. Over the last 30 years Nesse has become the main driving force for the development of evolutionary explanations for mental health disorders, hence we will consider his ideas in some detail.

WHY ARE WE VULNERABLE TO MENTAL HEALTH PROBLEMS?

Many assume that evolutionary processes lead to organisms becoming perfectly adapted to their environment. As Randolph Nesse has pointed out, however, evolutionary psychologists do not assume that all human traits are adapted to the current social and environmental challenges. In fact, one of the central tenets of evolutionary medicine is that, due to limitations of evolutionary processes, there is a whole series of reasons why we are vulnerable to health-related problems (Nesse 2019). Nesse has outlined six kinds of evolutionary reasons for our vulnerability to illness (both physical and psychological):

1. Because our bodies (and minds) evolved during the Pleistocene, there is a mismatch between our current adaptations and the modern environment which we have recently created.
2. Pathogens (bacteria and viruses) evolve much faster than we (their hosts) can (think of COVID-19).
3. There are constraints on what natural selection can achieve.
4. There are evolutionary trade-offs which means that improving one trait can lead to imperfections in another trait.
5. Sometimes natural (and sexual) selection increase reproduction at the cost of health and longevity.
6. Many defensive responses have negative aspects (e.g. pain and anxiety).

Given that all bar number two have direct bearings on mental health issues, with the exception of parasites-related conditions, much of the remainder of this chapter will be devoted to a consideration of each of these in turn.

MISMATCH HYPOTHESIS

In contrast to our hominin ancestors, for many living in the industrialised parts of the world, today's diseases are a result of having too many resources rather than too few. These include diabetes, obesity, and lung and heart disease (Gluckman et al. 2016; Nesse 2019). All four of these are the result of overindulgence combined with a sedentary lifestyle. While, virtually all of us living in the developed parts of the globe have more comfortable lives than those living in the few remaining forager societies (imagine living without a dentist or anaesthetics!), the latter very rarely suffer from the problems listed above. If we consider the lifestyles of current living forager societies such as the San bush people of Southern Africa, it is clear that they simply don't have the opportunity to over-indulge on sugar, fat and salt on a regular basis. Honey and ripe sugary fruit are unpredictable and patchy. Likewise, meat, when provided by hunters, is a luxury that may be gorged on by a tribe, but not every day (Lee 1979). While the lives of the San foragers are not identical to our Pleistocene ancestors, it is believed that (at least for those who have not been displaced by colonialists) their lives have remained largely unaltered for around

Figure 6.2 A group of San bush people on a foraging expedition

80,000 years. For these bush people, rather like all of our ancestors, an obese, sedentary lifestyle choice does not exist.

This mismatch between the ancestral and current environment does not, of course, relate only to food availability (and how sedentary we have become). As Nesse has pointed out, whereas we have used alcohol and even tobacco in some areas for a very long time, it is only in relatively recent years that these have become ubiquitous, leading to increases in health-related problems. Furthermore, in relation to mental health, as we disperse away from the support network of our nuclear family, rates of depression and anxiety have no doubt increased rapidly. More subtly, given the improved availability of nutrition, children grow up physically much faster than our ancient ancestors would have. This, in turn, can lead to physical development running ahead of psychological maturity. A case in point is the fact that girls today often begin menstruating by the age of 11 or 12 (Soliman, De Sanctis and Elalaily 2014). This no doubt can lead to inappropriate attention from older males in an increased likelihood of developing anxiety disorders. It might even help to explain the rise in anorexia nervosa (which pauses menstruation) in teenage girls.

BOX 6.3 DEPRESSION AND SOCIAL COMPARISON

Most depressive illnesses fall into one of two main categories – **major depressive disorder** and **bipolar depression** (Kring and Johnson 2019; Ray 2018). In bipolar depression, periods of low lethargic mood are interspersed with periods of highly energetic positive mood (mania, see later). In major depression, however periods of low mood are interspersed with periods of relatively stable mood. Although rates of bipolar depression have remained relatively unchanged over the last century, rates of major depression have risen rapidly ever since the end of the Second World War. This rise has been particularly associated with the more affluent countries than with the poorer ones (WHO 2008, 2012; Hidaka 2012; Twenge 2015). This finding raises the question of why should it be that successive generations living in the wealthier parts of the world appear to report higher rates of depression? Perhaps a version of the mismatch hypothesis known as the 'social comparison' explanation can

Figure 6.3 Amish wagons in Pennsylvania

help us out here. The social comparison explanation, suggests the rise of social media has made our world in effect shrink, leading to unrealistic social comparisons being made. The idea here is that we determine our self-esteem by comparing ourselves with others around us. During most of human evolution, making comparisons with members of our tribe would have led to a reasonable level of self-esteem, because no one would have had the sort of prestige, wealth and glamour that we see today via social media. Hence, we currently make very unrealistic comparisons, which would not have been possible during the Pleistocene. Even for the first half of the twentieth century, these idealised images would have been relatively rare. In recent years, however, those using social media have become bombarded with extraordinarily successful, glamorous images of, for example, supermodels, pop singers and movie stars. Such images, by comparison, can make our own lives seem quite mundane. Hence, according to social comparison theory, our feeling of self-esteem can become lowered to the point where many experience a state of depression. Interestingly, studies of those communities living in post-industrialised states, but who have rejected modern developments (including social media), such as the Amish, report much lower rates of depression than their modern-living counterparts (Ilardi et al. 2007; Ilardi 2010).

EVOLUTIONARY CONSTRAINTS

One of the great surprises for students of evolution is the realisation that, in addition to problems of mismatch, there are a number of other constraints on perfection. For one thing, evolutionary change has to take place within the context of existing adaptations. An example of this is the fact that, while bipedal locomotion (walking upright rather than 'on all fours') has many advantages (such as freeing up the hands) it also means that back problems are rife within our species. Millions of years of quadrupedal locomotion, followed by a lengthy period of knuckle walking, has left us with a back that really is not ideal for bipedal locomotion. The point is that progressive increases in upright walking provided more opportunities than challenges. This means that natural selection favoured this method of locomotion but did not go so far as to perfect it. (Note this can also be seen as an evolutionary 'trade-off' problem – see next section.) A second problem is sex. Like it or loath it, if we want to pass our genes on directly then we can only do so by sexual reproduction. As we saw earlier, this involves randomly throwing away half of our genes and combining the remaining 50 per cent with another person. So, gene combinations are continually being broken up each time we breed. It's not perfect but it seems to work (and people seem to like it, see Chapter 2). A third problem is that many adaptations are polygenic traits (see earlier and Chapter 1). This means they rely on a number of genes acting in harmony. This also means that some people will not have all of the genes necessary to develop that trait appropriately. Evolutionary psychologists think these three constraints on perfection help us to understand why our species is riddled with affective disorders. An example of this is the existence of anxiety disorders.

It does not take a great deal of imagination to realise that being able to experience anxiety is a useful adaptation. (Being unable to feel anxiety in the presence of aggressive strangers or fierce predators does not make for a good survival strategy!). Given, however, anxiety is almost certainly a polygenic trait, this means that some people, due in part to the mixture of genes they inherit, experience too much and some too little of it. While having too little clearly is a bad strategy, having too much might keep you safe but at a huge cost of missed opportunities. (Note, this has parallels with extreme extraversion and introversion discussed earlier). Hence people who find themselves at the extreme anxious end of the distribution are likely to be classified as having an anxiety disorder. Common anxiety disorders include social anxiety disorder (where people find speaking in front of others highly stressful), separation anxiety disorder (where people feel very anxious if left alone) and phobias such as arachnophobia (fear of spiders). These are considered to be disorders when the level of anxiety is debilitating, as is the case for around 16.6 per cent of Europeans (Somers et al. 2006). It is likely that anxiety disorders are maintained in a population, in part, simply because they are polygenic traits leading to a normal distribution in levels of anxiety. It is worth noting at this point, that, in addition to constraints on what natural selection can do, this high proportion of sufferers is likely to have been exacerbated by features of the modern environment such as crowded cities and fear-inducing news stories that would not have existed during the Pleistocene. That is, the mismatch hypothesis also plays into constraints on perfection. Note, also, that, in addition to anxiety disorder, the high level of depressive disorders can also be explained by such constraints.

EVOLUTIONARY DESIGN TRADE-OFFS

As Nesse has pointed out:

> The body is a bundle of trade-offs ... Your brain could be bigger but at the risk of death during childbirth ... Your blood pressure could be lower, at the cost of weaker, slower movement ... You could be less sensitive to pain, at the cost of being injured more often.
>
> (Nesse 2019, p. 39)

In addition to physical design trade-offs we appear to have psychological ones as well. Consider bipolar disorder (formally known as 'manic depression'). As mentioned above, sufferers have periods of deep depression interspersed with periods of manic mood. For some, during the periods of **mania**, their symptoms overlap with those of another serious psychological disorder – schizophrenia. In both cases sufferers may hold false (sometimes grandiose) beliefs, experience paranoia or even hear voices. Also, interestingly, bipolar disorder and schizophrenia tend to cluster in families, suggesting they may be related to common underlying genes (Craddock, O'Donovan and Owen 2005). Some evolutionary psychiatrists consider bipolar disorders may be kept in the population due to an evolutionary design trade-off. American clinical psychologist Kay Redfield Jamison has an intriguing suggestion as to what the positive features of this trade-off might be. Jamison (1993, 2011) examined a large number of highly successful artists, poets and musicians and discovered an astonishingly high rate of bipolar disorder. Overall, she found that, while 1 per cent of the general population has bipolar disorder, the figure for highly artistically talented people is around 38 per cent. Examples of the famously artistic people now believed to have had bipolar disorder include Vincent van Gogh, William Blake, Edgar Allen Poe, Sylvia Plath, Robert Schumann, Ernest Hemingway and Virginia Woolf.

Interestingly, in addition to this astonishingly high rate of bipolar disorder, Jamison also found that, during their manic phase, sufferers use three times as much alliteration and idiosyncratic, rhyming words in their speech than the general population (Jamison 1993). Because of this she suggests it is the creativity of the manic phase that maintains bipolar disorder within our species. In our ancestral past, having a family member who has sudden creative insight and develops novel ways of doing things, such as use of fire and ways of tracking prey, may well have more than compensated for their periods of depression. Perhaps in some way, as Jamison has suggested, the depression is the price they pay for such creativity? It should be noted that high levels of creativity have also been observed in individuals diagnosed with schizophrenia. Unfortunately, they are frequently quite disorganised, making this explanation less likely. We will consider schizophrenia later on.

REPRODUCTION FAVOURED OVER HEALTH AND LONGEVITY

It's easy to fall into the trap of thinking that natural selection selects for a longer, healthier life. Under some circumstances this does appear to be the case; just think of anti-predator adaptations, such as improved visual acuity and faster legs to help improve escape. In such cases it certainly helps if you are healthy and having the ability to avoid predators clearly extends life expectancy. These are,

Figure 6.4 Self-portrait of Vincent van Gogh (1887), the Dutch post-impressionist painter who is generally regarded to have suffered from bipolar depression and took his own life in 1890 at the age of 37

however, side issues. Natural selection selects for maximum transmission of genes and while this might extend life span and health with regard to, say, predator avoidance, it can also reduce both health and longevity. A case in point is the 50 per cent of the human population who have a much-reduced life expectancy when compared with the other half. If you haven't guessed it already, we are talking about males. While males generally have greater muscular strength than females, in all other respects they are the weaker sex (see Chapter 2). On average men live seven years less than women and during their teens and early twenties they are three times more likely to die than their female counterparts (Kruger and Nesse 2006). What causes this huge difference? In a word – testosterone. In young men, testosterone suppresses the immune system (and is one of the main reasons men have significantly higher rates of death from cancer) and simultaneously increases risk-taking behaviour. Often this involves direct competition with other males. They do this because, as we saw in Chapter 2, females invest more in the production of offspring leading to male/male competition. Hence, while high circulating testosterone has evolved to help males pass on their genes, counter-intuitively, it also shortens their lives. Male mammals in general are 'live fast, die young' strategists. This is because the male mammalian strategy generally leads to the insemination of more females, when they are successful in male/male competition. Humans are somewhat different in that we are a pair-bonding species (by-and-large) and it no doubt paid our male ancestors to survive to increase the chances of offspring survival. Despite this, they still succumb to the effects of their testosterone at a substantially younger age than women. We can think of this as the reproductive cost to males. This is simple evidence that natural selection is not necessarily about increasing health and longevity.

Before we start to feel too sorry for men and their reproductive costs, we should also consider the reproductive costs to women. While they live on average to a significantly older age than men, the costs of giving birth are, of course, enormous and there is always the risk of death in childbirth. Thankfully for much of the planet, death in childbirth is now relatively rare. But it still occurs in all nations.

DEFENCE RESPONSES WITH NEGATIVE ASPECTS

Fever, diarrhoea, pain, coughing, lethargy and nausea. What do all of these symptoms have in common? Yes, they are all unpleasant symptoms of contagious disease; but they are also all defensive responses designed by natural selection to protect us from the pathogens that are attempting to invade our bodies. These unpleasant symptoms, which our own bodies are creating, make life difficult for us because they are designed to make life difficult for the bugs. Lethargy is due to the removal of much of our iron from the bloodstream and into the liver. Vomiting and coughing are attempts to expel the pathogen, while raising your body temperature helps to kill off viruses and bacteria as they can only survive within a narrow range of temperatures. Interestingly, as Nesse himself has pointed out, if not too severe, it might speed up recovery if we let these symptoms persist for a while before considering medical intervention. Often, especially in the West, at the first sign of such symptoms our GP prescribes medications that help to boost iron and reduce temperature. Clinicians frequently perceive such symptoms as abnormalities rather than as traits that are designed to aid recovery – a position that Nesse calls the **clinician's illusion** (Nesse 2005). This means that 'just what the Doctor ordered' is just what suits the bug. Of course, this idea of 'let things be' for a while is a tricky game to play. Research does suggest, however, that the rate of recovery can be speeded up when symptoms are allowed to continue for a while (Nesse 2005). Interestingly the clinician's illusion may also be true for mental health issues. Some evolutionary psychologists have suggested that what we consider today to be psychiatric disorders might have arisen, in part, as a result of our body's defence mechanisms (Nesse 2019).

BOX 6.4 DO PEOPLE INHERIT DEPRESSION?

As with many maladies, it has been observed that both main forms of depression (major and bipolar) appear to cluster in families (Ray 2018). But does this prove that depression is inherited? The problem with jumping to this conclusion is that many non-genetic problems also run in families. A clear example of this is poverty. We would not assume that, because a number of members of a family live in poverty, this has been genetically inherited. One method that has been used to test the degree to which genes might be involved in depression is to compare concordance rates for depression for the two types of twins that naturally occur – mono- and dizygotic. (Note that concordance, in this context, refers to the probability, represented as a percentage, that two related individuals will both have a particular characteristic.) Because monozygotic twins share 100 per cent of their genes, while dizygotic ones only share 50 per cent by common descent, then when the former show significantly higher concordance rates than the latter, it is suggestive that genes are strongly involved in differences for the trait. Elliot Gershon and co-researchers compared concordance rates for mono- and dizygotic twins for both bipolar and major depression. The team uncovered clear evidence that there is a relationship between the genes we inherit and the likelihood of developing depressive illness. As we can see in Table 6.2, monozygotic twins have significantly higher concordance rates.

Table 6.2 Concordance rates for two forms of depression in twin studies

Type of twin	*Bipolar depression*	*Major depression*
Monozygotic (100% of genes shared)	70%	40%
Dizygotic (50% of genes shared)	34%	11%

Source: from Gerson et al. 1990.

Interestingly, however, while having a relative with major depression somewhat increases the chances of developing the disorder oneself, having a relative with bipolar depression greatly increases the chances of developing the disorder (Gershon et al. 1990). Hence bipolar disorder has a higher heritability than major depression. This might suggest it is maintained in our species as an adaptation.

In the case of mental health problems, some evolutionary psychologists have suggested enduring extreme emotional states such as depression, while being unpleasant (rather like fever), may have arisen to make us withdraw from activity at times when it would increase survival chances such as following attack. (Depressed people frequently lack energy and abstain from normal energy-sapping activities.) Under such circumstances it may have paid our ancestors to recoup before engaging in normal activities once more. Some have suggested such a state would most likely have passed more rapidly than today because the source of the depression is unlikely to remain long term (unlike today when say you have a bullying boss who remains in place). Although this sounds rather theoretical, it does have some research support. Matthew Keller and Randolph Nesse (2006) found that different kinds of depressive problems led to different types of depressive symptoms.

For example, in a group of 445 participants, loss of partner was seen to lead to emotional pain, crying and requests for comforting social support, whereas failure in an enterprise led to pessimistic exhaustion. In the case of the former type of depression, reaching out for help may well be an adaptive response, whereas for the latter, withdrawal from energy sapping activities might also prove adaptive. Hence, it may pay clinicians to consider the adaptive response of different types of depression. This might, of course, also be true for long-term anxiety issues. Note, this form of explanation overlaps with the mismatch hypothesis.

BOX 6.5 IS THERE AN EVOLUTIONARY EXPLANATION FOR PSYCHOPATHY?

Psychopathic individuals show a callous disregard for the rights of other people. They are manipulative and antisocial, lacking in empathy and remorse. Think of Adolf Hitler, Saddam Hussein, Harvey Weinstein, Wayne Cousins and Vladimir Putin – you get the picture. In a nutshell, they are extremely unpleasant people (and usually male). Cross-cultural studies suggest psychopathic individuals are found in all cultures (Babiak and Hare 2019). Given that, as we have seen, much of human social behaviour is based around acts of reciprocal altruism, how might evolutionists explain the existence of psychopathy? Some evolutionists have turned the argument that reciprocation is so commonplace on its head to suggest why psychopathy is maintained within human populations. According to the **cheater hypothesis**, where rates of cooperative behaviour are high (as is generally the case in human populations), it may pay a small proportion of a given population to develop a free-rider strategy where you reap the benefits without paying the costs (Frank 1988; Mealey 1995; Taylor and Workman 2023). This may be a part-and-parcel of **frequency dependent selection** (FDS). That is, cheating only works when the vast majority are broadly reciprocators. The notion that psychopathy might have evolved as an alternate FDS strategy is supported by three findings, First, it occurs in a little over 1 per cent of the population (it only works if it is rare); second, there is clear evidence that it is at least partly heritable; third and finally, individuals diagnosed as psychopaths are reproductively successful (Taylor and Workman 2023).

THE ENIGMA OF SCHIZOPHRENIA

Schizophrenia is the most serious of psychotic disorders. It affects around 1 per cent of the world's population and this proportion is invariant between nations. As referred to above, schizophrenia is characterised by delusions, hallucinations and disordered thought (Troisi 2020). Heritability of the illness is high, around 60–80 per cent, and fecundity is reduced (Srinivasan et al. 2016). Putting these three facts together, that is, it is debilitating, it reduces reproductive output and yet it is highly heritable has led to it being labelled an 'evolutionary enigma' (Burns 2007). So how might evolutionists explain its worldwide existence? Over the last 20 years, evidence has accumulated that a large number of genes are involved in the development of schizophrenia. Today, a number of experts have converged on a broadly similar evolutionary explanation. This is the notion that the illness is a by-product of the relatively recent evolution of human language and creative thinking (Burns 2007; Srinivasan et al. 2016; Plomin 2018). The idea here is that selective pressures for language and creative thinking led to a brain that requires numerous genes to work in harmony during development, increasing the possibility of these abilities developing abnormally. The evidence is somewhat indirect but is based on the fact that people with schizophrenia do show abnormal brain activity and that the genes (more than 100) known to be associated with the disorder have arisen quite recently in human evolution, coinciding with the evolution of language and complex reasoning (Srinivasan et al. 2016). In a nutshell, the wiring is now so complex that, in around one in a hundred, an abnormal pattern of neurological networks is established. No doubt, in addition to the gene combination people inherit, this is also due, in part, to stressful early life events the dance between genes and environment plays out.

BOX 6.6 DO INDIVIDUALS WITH AUTISM HAVE NEUROLOGICAL ADVANTAGES?

Autism is a neurodevelopmental condition that affects around one in 100 people. Autistic individuals experience difficulties with social interactions, repetitive behaviours and highly focused interests.

Figure 6.5 Swedish environmental activist Greta Thunberg

Today it is generally considered as a spectrum disorder (autism spectrum disorder – ASD) meaning people vary from highly skilled to severely challenged. Although they generally have difficulties relating to others, due to their intensely focused interests, some experts have begun to suggest autistic people may have advantages that allow them to outperform neurotypical people in certain settings. A case in point is neuropsychiatrist Laurent Mottron of the University of Montreal who not only studies the abilities of people 'on the autism spectrum' but also employs them as his co-researchers, precisely because of these abilities. In particular, Mottron has found that high functioning autistics exceed non-autistics in their ability to process large bodies of perceptual information and, because of their intensely focussed interests, they are also less likely to give up on issues that are important to them. This might help to explain why Swedish climate change activist Greta Thunberg (Figure 6.5), who has been diagnosed with high functioning autism, has been so successful in getting other young (and older) people, to engage with environmental issues. To Mottron, rather than simply being a psychological disability, ASD might be maintained in our species due to the advantages it bestows. In his words 'often, autistic behaviours, although atypical, are still adaptive' (Mottron 2011, p. 3).

This conception of the development of schizophrenia raises the question, how might we relate this to the five evolutionary explanations examined above? With regard to the mismatch hypothesis, it is worth mentioning the recent rapid changes in the physical and social environment that our species has created may well have introduced new risk factors that increase the likelihood of the disorder developing. Such rapid changes might, for example, include living largely anonymous impersonal lives in enormous towns and cities when compared with the Pleistocene. Considering 'evolutionary constraints' and 'trade-offs', the idea of recent changes in the genes involved in brain development may well be a good example of both of these (they are, after all, overlapping explanations). This means it may be a 'trade-off' as the cost some pay for the general evolution of a complex brain and an evolutionary constraint in that there is simply not sufficient positive selection to rid our species of this problem. When, however, we consider 'reproduction over health' and 'defensive responses', these appear to be the least likely ways of explaining the continued existence of this serious psychotic disorder.

Hence, like the affective disorders involving anxiety and depressive illness, our understanding of psychotic disorder such as schizophrenia may also benefit from a knowledge of the limitations and constraints that ancient recurrent selection pressures have left our species with.

SUMMARY

Many psychologists who study individual differences today suggest there are five main factors or dimensions to personality: openness–closedness, conscientiousness–unconscientiousness, extraversion–introversion, agreeableness–disagreeableness and neuroticism–stability. Each of these 'big five' factors has a relatively high level of heritability (varying from 0.35 to 0.5), suggesting almost half of the variation between people in these personality factors is accounted for by genetic differences between them. There are both benefits and costs associated with having high or low levels of each of the big five. For example, being high on extraversion is associated with having a larger number of sexual partners, while being low on this dimension is associated with being more likely to 'play safe' in relationships. Evolutionary psychologists have proposed a number of hypotheses to explain individual differences within an evolutionary framework. Frequency-dependent selection suggests it may pay individuals to act differently to the majority. An example of this is a personality that makes free riding more likely in a population where most people are relatively altruistic. Random variation around the mean results from re-combining genes during sexual reproduction. This random variation helps to explain why people vary in terms of personality factors. Reactive heritability is based on the notion that we all receive feedback from others based largely on our physical appearance. Hence, a physically robust boy learns that other boys are likely to give way to him and this, in turn, can lead him down the path of being more extravert. Finally, Frank Sulloway has suggested birth order effects lead to individual differences as each child takes on a different 'ecological role' within the family.

In recent years, evolutionists have begun to explore the relationship between ancient selective pressures and modern-day psychological health issues. Randolph Nesse has outlined six reasons why we are particularly vulnerable to mental health issues. These are: the notion that there is mismatch between our current adaptations and the modern environment; the fact that pathogens evolve faster than we do; there are constraints on what evolution can do; evolution of some traits can lead to imperfections in other traits; reproduction can lead to health costs and some defensive responses have negative aspects. Affective disorders involving anxiety and depression may be more prevalent today than in the past due to novel pressures that our ancestors did not encounter in the ancient past. These include inappropriate social comparisons, which can lead to a lowering of self-esteem. Among creative people there are high rates of bipolar depression, which involves periods of depression interspersed with periods of manic mood. Kay Redfield Jamison has suggested this creativity is the selective advantage which maintains this form of depression within human populations. The serious psychotic disorder schizophrenia, which involves disordered and delusional thought, may be maintained in our species as a side effect of the recent evolution of a greatly enlarged brain to support language and creative thought.

FURTHER READING

Abed, R. and St John-Smith, P. (2022) *Evolutionary Psychiatry: Current Perspectives on Evolution and Mental Health*. Cambridge: Cambridge University Press.

Buss, D. M. and Hawley, P. (2011) *The Evolution of Personality and Individual Differences*. Oxford: Oxford University Press.

Del Giudice, M. (2018) *Evolutionary Psychopathology: A Unified Approach*. New York, NY: Oxford University Press.

Nesse, R. M. (2019) *Good Reasons for Feeling Bad: Insights from the Frontier of Evolutionary Psychiatry*. London: Allen Lane.

Ray, W. J. (2018) *Abnormal Psychology: Neuroscience Determinants of Human Behavior and Experience* (2nd edn). Thousand Oaks, CA: Sage.

Sternberg, R. J. (2021) *Adaptive Intelligence: Surviving and Thriving in Times of Uncertainty*. Cambridge: Cambridge University Press.

7

EVOLUTION, CULTURE AND LANGUAGE

WHAT IS CULTURE?

To many people, culture is associated with civilisation: classical music, say, great works of literature, or high art such as paintings or sculpture – you know, the things you feel that you are supposed to like. If you did think that, then you are absolutely correct, at least in the historical sense. The Romans first used the term culture in this sense because they thought that high art 'cultivated' or improved a person in a similar way to the way that farmers cultivate their crops through agriculture ('agri' being Latin for 'field'). From this rather high-minded definition the German philosopher and historian Samuel von Pufendorf changed the meaning slightly to mean 'refers to all the ways in which human beings overcome their original barbarism, and through artifice, become fully human' (Velkley 2002). And so culture became what it means today in the social sciences, all those things that clothe our naked humanity including our beliefs, language, rituals, artefacts and, well, our clothes.

In addition to this, many researchers explicitly define culture as something that is learned rather than innate. For example, the anthropologist E. A. Hoebel (1966) defines culture as 'the integrated system of learned behavior patterns which are characteristic of the members of a society and which are not the result of biological inheritance'. Many other social scientists followed this definition, for example, Carter and Qureshi (1995) similarly define culture as 'a learned system of meaning and behavior that is passed from one generation to the next'.

The study of culture in psychology is bound up with study of cultural differences. Today psychologists understand the way that

DOI: 10.4324/9780429274428-7

different peoples behave as being influenced, in part, by their culture. This wasn't always the case, and it is instructive to examine a little bit of history in order to understand why things are the way they are now.

A BRIEF HISTORY OF CULTURE

In the Western world, at least, the fascination with other cultures began in the eighteenth century's 'Age of Discovery' when explorers such as Captain James Cook and Wilhelm von Humboldt travelled the globe encountering cultures that differed greatly from those found in Europe at the time. On finding that the technology of these peoples was often considerably less advanced than that of the Europeans, the conclusion was frequently drawn that this was because their minds were also less advanced. The otherwise great German biologist Ernst Haeckel – and he was by no means alone in expressing this view – stated that 'natural men are closer to the higher vertebrates than to highly civilised Europeans' (Richards 1986).

This view changed in the late nineteenth and early twentieth century when anthropologists from the **cultural relativist school** established by Franz Boas (1852–1942) such as Margaret Mead argued that this biological determinist perspective was entirely the wrong way round. It wasn't the people that made the culture, rather it was the culture that made the people. The sociologist Ellsworth Faris summed up this position when he wrote in 1927 that: 'Instincts do not create customs; customs create instincts, for the putative instincts of human beings are always learned, never native' (quoted in Degler 1991, p. 161).

So, who is correct? Does culture create people or do people create culture? Perhaps unsurprisingly the answer is 'both'. Some insight into the subtleties of the debate can be seen by looking at research on **cultural universals**.

ARE THERE CULTURAL UNIVERSALS?

There is a story of an argument between two men called Donald: Donald Brown a cultural anthropologist and Donald Symons an evolutionary anthropologist. Brown, at the time of their disagreement, was very much schooled in cultural relativism, believing that cultures were not tied to biology and were thus free to vary from place to place and time to time, with the result that all cultures were in some way unique. Symons, on the other hand believed that culture was partly a manifestation of an underlying innate human psychology and, as a result, each culture would share many characteristics with other cultures. Brown disagreed profoundly and bet Symons (it is not clear how much the bet was for, or even if there was money involved) that he could show that each culture had its own unique signature and, crucially, there would be no one thing that existed in all cultures. Brown studied the anthropological records which is basically a database of cultural traits from a large number of different societies – industrial, agricultural and hunter–gatherer – from across the globe, certain that he would prove Symonds wrong and show that there was nothing that was common to all cultures.

He lost the bet.

Against all of his background and training he was forced to acknowledge that there *were* in fact universals, but at least he got a book out of it. In *Human Universals* (Brown 1991) he detailed over 200 different cultural universals with many more added since. A sample is shown in Table 7.1.

One thing that needs to be made clear is that these universals are pitched at quite a general level. For example, moral sentiments exist in all cultures, but this by no means suggests that such sentiments are identical in all cultures. We can say the same about many others such as death rituals and rites of passage, the specifics of which vary widely. On the other hand, some are much more uniform cross-culturally, such as recognition of people by face, thumb sucking and tickling.

A second thing that should be pointed out is that no claim is made that *every* person in a given culture adheres to *all* universals, just that they are practised widely within those cultures. Not everyone gets married, believes in the supernatural or is wary around snakes, after all.

Furthermore, if we adopt the definition discussed above that cultural practices are learned from other people then some of these don't fit. It is unlikely that the tendency for right-handedness, the preference to recognise people by their face (rather than, say smell)

Table 7.1 Just some of Brown's cultural universals

aesthetics	sexual jealousy
belief in supernatural/religion	sexual modesty
body adornment	incest, prevention or avoidance
childbirth customs	males more aggressive
childcare	marriage
copulation normally conducted in private	medicine
cooking with fire	melody
crying	moral sentiments
customary greetings	mourning
dance	murder prohibited
death rituals	myths
division of labour by sex	poetry/rhetoric
fear of death	preference for own children and close kin
gossip	recognising people by their face
husband older than wife on average	snakes, wariness around
In-group favouritism	socialisation includes toilet training
pretend play	special speech for special occasions
pride	statuses and roles
rape (and rape prohibited)	tabooed foods
revenge	tabooed utterances
recognition of individuals by face	territoriality
right-handedness as population norm	thumb sucking
rites of passage	tickling
rituals	tools
sexual attraction	

or childcare fall into this category. But many of them do seem to be acquired, or at least modified from others such as tabooed foods, body adornment and poetry.

THE RELATIONSHIP BETWEEN EVOLUTION AND CULTURAL UNIVERSALS

Broadly speaking, Brown's cultural universals fall into four categories: those where cultural learning is unlikely to have had much influence in their development – the aforementioned preference for recognising others by their faces but also others from Brown's list such as feeling pain. On the other hand, some seem to be purely cultural: cooking with fire, for example, exists in all cultures but is unlikely to have any specific biological origins and can thus be considered a purely cultural phenomenon with people either discovering it themselves, or learning from other cultures who use fire in this way (we will have more to say about cooking later).

The third category are those that are likely to have had direct evolutionary benefits. Incest avoidance, for example, is a useful mechanism for avoiding mating with close relatives and therefore risking passing on dangerous recessive genes to offspring. Most toxic genes are recessive (needing two copies of the same gene to express the trait) and relatively uncommon, but the likelihood that someone has the copy of the *same* toxic gene as you goes up alarmingly the more closely related they are to you. In-group biases are another with possible direct advantages (see Chapter 3).

Finally, some have less obvious evolutionary advantages and may be a bi-product of other evolved processes – thumb sucking is likely to be a hangover from the comfort-giving and evolutionarily vital infant activity of suckling. Likewise, Steven Pinker (1997) argues that, despite being universal, music and poetry confer no evolutionary advantage but are side effects of our language processing ability which is sensitive to pitch, rhythm and prosody. He suggests that music is like cheesecake which we enjoy despite not evolving a preference specifically for cheesecake.

> We evolved circuits that gave us trickles of enjoyment from the sweet taste of ripe fruit, the creamy mouthfeel of fats and oils from nuts ... Cheesecake ... is a megadose of agreeable stimuli which we concocted for the express purpose of pressing our pleasure buttons.
>
> (Pinker 1997, pp. 524–525)

Music, he argues, is also artificially produced to push out 'pleasure buttons' and, in his opinion, has no adaptive value in the EEA, although, it might do now.

DID CULTURE EVOLVE?

There are two meanings to the question 'did culture evolve' the first is simply whether culture changes over time, to which the answer is an obvious yes. It hardly needs saying that over time there has been an increase in cultural complexity in terms of our institutions (democracy, the rule of law, education systems and so on) and our technologies (computers, transport, medicine) to name but two areas. Culture builds on culture and ideas beget new ideas so in this sense culture has evolved and continues to do so (see Pinker for a discussion of whether these changes are for the good, or otherwise). The other sense of the question, and one that is more relevant to a book on evolutionary psychology, is whether the ability to acquire, generate, use and transmit culture is something that evolved, and most thinkers would seem to answer this question in the affirmative also.

DOES CULTURE HAVE A PURPOSE, AND IF SO WHAT?

Although culture is very probably not unique to humans (see Box 7.1), human culture is, by comparison, off the scale.

BOX 7.1 KEY CONCEPTS: DO NON-HUMAN ANIMALS HAVE CULTURE?

At first the idea of non-human animals having culture might seem a little crazy – especially if we consider culture in its non-technical sense (see earlier) as describing art, music and literature. On the other hand, if we define culture as relating to non-heritable behaviour that is acquired by social learning, it begins to seem more plausible that non-humans might also have culture.

The most obvious place to look would be our closest relatives, the chimpanzees, and research has shown that chimpanzees do indeed seem to have culture. Whiten et al. (1999) have shown that there are many variations among different groups of chimpanzees that are not reducible to mere biology. For example, some groups of chimps use tools to pick termites from their mounds and others rocks to crack nuts and each group has different methods of doing this, suggesting that these practices are copied from other group members.

Another (less closely related) primate, the Japanese macaque, has learned to wash sweet potatoes in order to remove unpalatable grit (Kawai 1965). They are also known to engage in snowball fights in the winter. Both of these habits appear to be learned from one another. Outside of mammals, many avian species are known to acquire at least part of their song by imitating other birds around

Figure 7.1 A Japanese macaque with a snowball

them (Catchpole and Slater 2008), something that has led people to claim they have developed regional dialects (Catchpole and Slater 2008).

So what might be the purpose of culture? Robert Boyd and Peter Richerson (Richerson and Boyd 2008; Boyd, Richerson and Henrich 2011) have proposed that the ability to acquire culture evolved through a process of natural selection to help us cope with rapid environmental change. During the last 2.6 million years the earth has been in the grip of an ice age, although for the past 10,000 years or so the grip has loosened somewhat, as the permanent ice has now retreated and permanently resides only in the polar regions or on the loftiest of mountains.

During this period there have been periods of comparative warmth, as now, punctuated by periods where ice sheets have covered the northern parts of North America and Northern Europe. Many organisms adapted to these conditions through a process of natural selection, for example by evolving fur coats or, in the case of trees, needle-like leaves that enable them to shed snow more easily. Boyd and Richerson suggest our ancestors evolved the ability to create culture including the ability for intellectual innovation and the ability to learn these innovations from one another rapidly. This theory is called **dual inheritance theory** because they propose that in addition to the standard means of inheritance – through genes – humans have acquired a second means of inheritance, which is to acquire culture from our elders. If Boyd and Richerson are correct and there was a strong evolutionary pressure on humans that supercharged our ability to acquire culture, relative to other animals (see Box 7.1), this should be reflected in our psychology. This is what we discuss next.

THE PSYCHOLOGICAL MECHANISMS THAT UNDERLIE CULTURE

In 1931 Winthrop and Luella Kellogg had a new addition to their family to accompany their ten-month old son Donald. Gua was a 7½-month-old female chimpanzee born in captivity in Havana, Cuba. Winthrop was a behavioural scientist with the belief that our environment makes us what we are. This view was reinforced by stories in the 1920s on two Indian children who had supposedly been raised by wolves and exhibited typical wolf behaviour (scratching, biting, eating raw meat and so on). To test this hypothesis Gua was raised alongside Donald and treated exactly the same as him. To begin with Gua did well, sometimes doing better than Donald in some tasks despite being two and a half months his junior (Kellogg & Kellogg, 1933). She was more proficient at eating using a spoon and was able to follow simple commands given by her 'parents' more effectively than her 'brother'. Nine months on, the experiment was brought to an end, not just because after a promising start Gua had stalled in her ability to acquire human characteristics, but because Donald was starting to acquire chimpanzee characteristics including running about on all fours and bellowing the 'pant-hoot' of an excited chimpanzee: Gua was not imitating Donald, Donald was imitating Gua!

We are often disposed to be somewhat dismissive of imitation using pejorative words such as plagiarising or bootlegging. We also use colloquial phrases that cast imitation as something subhuman – 'parroting', for example or 'aping'. But as we have seen and will see in more detail, humans are much better at aping than apes.

Michael Tomasello (2014) lists some of the cognitive adaptations that permit human-style culture when compared to our chimpanzee relatives:

Imitation. Research by Nagell, Olguin and Tomasello (1993) reveals that adult chimps have the imitative ability of a two-year-old human. At least one reason why humans have this advantage is that they are capable of not just representing the *actions* of another, but can also represent their *goals*. Or to put it another way, as well as being able to determine *what* someone is doing, they can also determine *why* they are doing it. If someone assembles a collection of sticks in order to reach a piece of fruit and the person drops one of the pieces, a human child will realise that this is a mistake and omit the dropping when it comes to their turn. Chimps include the dropping stage, suggesting that they find it difficult to decide which actions matter and which do not (Tomasello 1999). Conversely, if children perceive there to be no obvious mistakes, then they will copy even apparently purposeless actions in what is known as **over-imitation** (Lyons, Young and Keil 2007). This is even more pronounced if children perceive there to be no obvious goal to the action, in which case, they imitate the actions much more closely. It is as if, in the absence of a goal, children assume that the sequence of actions *are* the goal. Some have even suggested that such imitation is the origin of ritualistic behaviour (Tennie, Call and Tomasello 2009).

Three-year-olds will also preferentially imitate someone from their in-group (e.g. speaks their own language, even when understanding language is not needed for imitation) over the out-group, confirming what we discussed in Chapter 3 about the importance of group-mindedness in our evolutionary history.

Sharing. Sharing and the sharing of food, in particular, is universal among humans. After a successful hunt, hunter–gatherers will share their spoils among members of the community. Even three-year-old children with resources that have been obtained by lucky accident shared about a third of their windfall with other children. Chimpanzees in a similar position never shared (Hamann et al. 2011). In the wild, when a chimpanzee catches a monkey, the spoils often make their way into the mouths of other chimps, but this is through a process whereby those not in position harass the possessor until he or she eventually relents.

Coordination. As just discussed, chimpanzees will sometimes as a group hunt monkeys for food. But in contrast to the delicately coordinated actions of human–hunters, this resembles a free-for-all in which a rabble of chimps chase the monkey through the undergrowth. One of the differences between humans and chimps is that they are able to represent a joint goal and each act in fulfilment of that goal in their own different ways. For example, even children as young as three will take up different roles in an experimental 'stag-hunt' game which has many of the characteristics of real hunting.

Conformity. Conformity, like imitation, is often seen as a negative trait exhibited by the uncreative mind. This is reinforced by the famous Solomon Asch (1951) conformity studies which show how people will apparently disbelieve the evidence of their own eyes by stating that a shorter line is more similar to a target line than one that is exactly the same (see Figure 7.2). While such instances are liable to have us throwing up our hands in profound embarrassment at our species, such examples constitute an important part of the evolution of human culture. Conformity to social norms ensures that people work together more effectively. An extreme example would be rules dictating which side of the road we drive

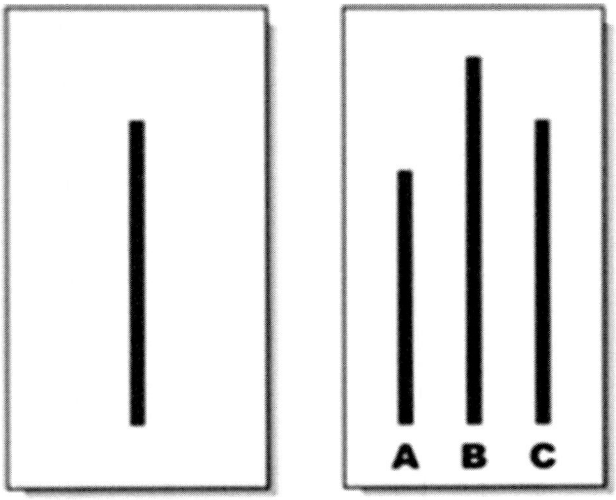

Figure 7.2 Stimuli from Asch's conformity studies. If a confederate states that the target line (on the left) is the same size as line A a surprising (one might say embarrassing) number of participants agree with them

on. It doesn't matter which side we choose, left or right, all that matters is that we all agree to drive on the same side. Other norms work towards boosting a common group identity, promoting social cohesion and **group-mindedness** (see Chapter 3), another aspect of human culture on Tomasello's list, as is our tendency to enforce social norms. From the age of three, children begin to enforce social norms and will issue sanctions to those who contravene them, for example if someone destroys someone else's property (Tomasello 2014).

Instruction. Finally, a huge difference between humans and non-humans is that humans engage in instructed learning (see later). Although chimpanzees and other primates participate in social learning (learn from each other), this has more in common with theft than a gift gladly given. A chimp may copy another chimp's actions if it feels it is useful, but a chimp will never offer direct instruction to another chimp.

GENE-CULTURE COEVOLUTION

Human cultural practices have left a mark on our genes. One of the simplest of these is lactose tolerance. You might know people who are lactose intolerant (you might even be lactose intolerant yourself). Lactose is a sugar found in milk and requires a special enzyme called lactase in order to digest it. Lacking this enzyme, lactose intolerant people become sick if they consume milk or some of its products. Although we, especially we in the West, consider lactose intolerance to be abnormal, it is actually lactose *tolerance* that is in need of explanation.

Milk, you see, is a foodstuff that is specifically designed to feed baby mammals before they are able to chew and digest real food for themselves. Once baby animals can eat a normal diet, the mother's milk dries up and the offspring's ability to produce lactase similarly evaporates.

Yet somehow *some* humans have avoided this switching off and can digest lactose in adulthood. Why? A clue can be found by looking at the ethnic origins of the people who can and can't consume milk. Most of the people who can digest milk have ancestors who kept cows, sheep and goats. We humans can't eat grass, which is a shame as there is and was a lot of it around, so people discovered that some animals can be used as a way of turning indigestible grass into food in the form of meat. You kill a cow just once, but if you use it as a way of turning grass into milk and its products (cheese, butter, yoghurt) the cow can supply you with food for all its life.

Because they had a more readily available food source, those people who were lactose tolerant were more likely to survive than those who were intolerant, so the gene for lactose tolerance spread through the populations that kept these kinds of animals (Bloom and Sherman, 2005), but not those who were more likely to keep chickens (which, being birds, do not produce milk) or pigs (which, being pigs, are pigs to milk).

A similar story of how cultural practices shaped human evolution starts with contaminated water. Water, then and now, frequently contains many pathogens that are potentially fatal. In 2017 the Global Burden of Disease estimated that 1.2 million people die per year as a direct result of drinking contaminated water (usually from treatable diseases such as diarrhoea). People in the West discovered that turning the water into ale killed many of the pathogens; in the East it was discovered that heating the water with herbs had a similar effect, in effect brewing tea. This is one of the reasons why people from the Far East tend to have lower tolerance to alcohol than those in the West.

Both of these examples serve to show that, as well as evolution influencing our ability to acquire culture (see above), culture itself has placed a selection pressure upon us, changing our biology. This is **gene-culture evolution** and its implication is that it is important to consider the influence of evolution on culture *and* the influence of culture on evolution if one is to obtain a more complete picture of our evolutionary past.

Our final example of the effects of culture on our genome is much more profound: cooking. No one knows exactly when cooking first arrived on the scene. The earliest date of which we can be certain is 300,000 BCE which is a very long time ago. Agriculture arrived around 12,000 years ago, remember (Shahack-Gross et al. 2014), whereas some push the date even further back into the mists of time. Primatologist Richard Wrangham (2009), for example, has argued that the cultural practice of cooking may have been discovered by one of our ancestors, *Homo erectus*.

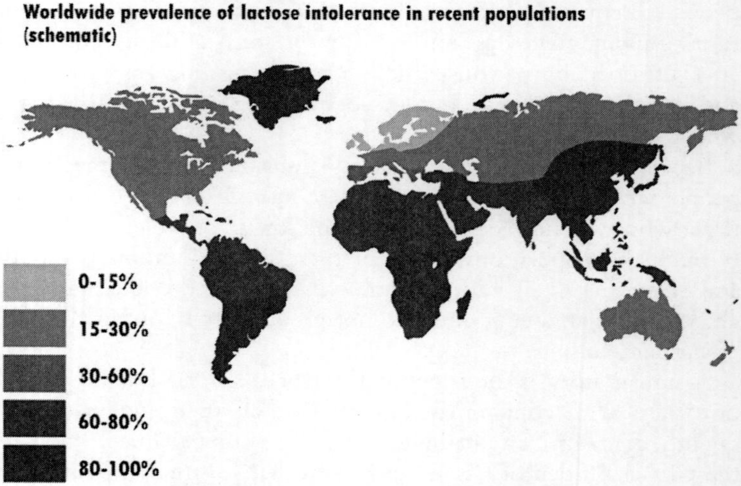

Figure 7.3 The distribution of lactose intolerance across the world

Whenever cooking was born, it seems to have had a profound effect on our evolution. Cooking food facilitates digestion, which means that our ancestors needed to spend far less time chewing and digesting food, freeing up time to do other things; humans spend much less of their day eating than their close relatives the chimpanzees. Cooking food also predigests it, which, according to Wrangham (2009), means that we can have a much more efficient gut in order to provide more energy to run a larger brain. So, more time, more brain power and, ultimately more specialisation, which is where we are going next.

THE ECONOMICS OF SPECIALISATION

The British biologist and writer, Matt Ridley (2010), posed the following problem:

> Imagine that there are two men called Adam and Oz. Adam takes four hours to make a spear and three hours to make an axe (which together amounts to seven hours). Oz, on the other hand, takes one

> hour to make a spear and two hours to make an axe (which together amounts to three hours). This means that Oz is better at making both spears and axes.

So the question is, does Oz need Adam?

Before reading on, try to answer the question yourself.

On the face of it would seem that Oz does not need Adam as Adam is worse at making both spears and axes than Oz. You might, however, reconsider this answer because, although Oz is better than Adam at both tasks, he is *much* better at axes. So think what would happen if Oz could focus exclusively on spears and persuade Adam to focus on what he is best at (but still worse than Oz): axes. Oz could then make two spears in two hours (saving one hour) whereas Adam could make two axes in six hours (again, saving one hour). Once made they then trade, so each has an axe and each has a spear.

This is the logic of specialisation: it is always better to delegate tasks that you are less good at to focus on tasks that you are better at, *even if the person to whom you are delegating the task is worse than you!* And, no doubt, because you are specialising in one thing, you will probably become even more proficient at producing it (Ridley 2010).

SPECIALISATION AND A TRADE

Central to specialisation is, of course, trade. One cannot live on axes alone but one can exchange axes for food, shelter and other necessities and comforts that themselves are more likely to be produced by the skilled craftsperson than the ham-fisted dilletante. It has even been suggested that one of the reasons why our ancestors outcompeted Neanderthals in Northern Europe is due to the fact that we traded and they didn't. There is no evidence for Neanderthals engaging in trade, whereas there is plenty for contemporary humans (Gamble, 1999; Horan, Bulte and Shogren 2005).

Nowadays our species is so culturally specialised that, as we discussed in Chapter 3, no one person knows how to make very much from scratch. Even something as simple as a pencil.

BOX 7.2 INTERNATIONAL DIFFERENCES IN WEALTH

The cyberpunk author William Gibson is purported to have said that 'the future is already here, it's just not evenly distributed' and rarely has that been so true as in the so-called Age of Exploration from the 1400s to the 1600s. This is when predominantly European explorers with galleons, swords, canon and guns travelled the world seizing territory from indigenous people with only stone-age weapons to defend themselves with. Furthermore, as American writer Jared Diamond (1998) points out, along with their weapons and trinkets, Europeans also took with them a heady cocktail of diseases to which they had immunity but that were lethal to anyone else. But why was the future *so* unevenly distributed, and why in favour of the Europeans rather than people from Africa or the Americas?

Diamond attempts to answer the question by examining the early history of various civilisations. Agriculture first began in the fertile crescent, which is the area around modern-day Iraq. Why there, we might ask? Diamond suggests that Eurasia (Europe and Asia) happens to have had the right species of animals and plants for domestication. Animals such as cows, sheep, pigs, poultry and horses which could be used for food, or, in the case of some, to pull ploughs. And those ploughs helped in the production of Eurasian crops such as wheat, peas and various types of bean. This stands in marked contrast to Africa and North America where there were no domesticable animals, and to South America which only has the Llama and its relatives (although there were crops such as maize and potatoes in the Americas).

The habitable parts of Eurasia are also largely East–West in axis, the area is much wider than it is tall, this means that any crop or animal can be moved east or west with little change in climate. Africa and the Americas have a largely North–South axis, meaning that moving animals around the country (upwards or downwards, as it were) would lead to greater changes in climate and more problems for the beleaguered animals and plants that might well freeze, boil, drown or desiccate.

Hence, the existence of appropriate species for domestication and being at the 'correct' axis led to the development of agriculture. This, in turn, led to specialisation, which led to the building of ships, steel swords, infantry, cavalry, a navy, guns. Perhaps it also led to a desire to own much of the world in order to support Europe's burgeoning population and, arguably, its greed. Diamond's (1998) book, *Guns, Germs and Steel*, is named after the tools that enabled this colonisation to occur. The significance of guns and steel has already been dealt with but what about germs? Why was Europe so laced with deadly pathogens?

We can trace this back to the domestication of animals. Many of the most virulent diseases in history have leapt across the species barrier. Chicken pox, smallpox and influenza all came from domesticated animals. Hence, by accident, farming had produced one of the deadliest weapons of Eurasia: disease. Each time Eurasians colonised parts of the world, they often killed off as many people through the diseases they brought as they did with guns and swords. The people they invaded had no prior contact with these domestic animals and hence lacked natural immunity. If evidence were needed for the destructive nature of disease, the 'Spanish' influenza pandemic of 1928 claimed between 50 and 100 million people (3–5 per cent of Earth's population). Even today, many of the most virulent diseases such as forms of avian influenza emanate from pathogens that have crossed the species barrier through agriculture, often in China, where the inappropriately named Spanish flu epidemic originated and, of course, COVID-19.

THE FUTURE OF CULTURAL STUDIES

Much of mainstream psychology has failed to take much interest in culture. While recognising it does influence child development (see Chapter 6), it has tended to leave the study of culture to social scientists such as sociologists and anthropologists. If we are to fully understand human nature, then we feel this really needs to change. We hope that this chapter has helped you to see why. Most people who research these things agree that our brains have changed little in thousands of years, but in a relatively short time our species has gone from forager tribes living in relatively small communities of perhaps around 150 people (see Chapter 2) to latte drinking, sophisticates who have little idea what our food is, let alone where it came from and who killed it. These differences might only be on the surface, but what a surface, for good and, of course, for bad.

EVOLUTION AND LANGUAGE

Language is an extremely important part of human culture. It forms part of our many rituals and rites of passage; we use it to pray to our deities, give instructions, ask for directions and to argue, seduce, demand and schmooze. Although most researchers think that language is unique to humans, it might not have always been the case. Research on Neanderthal physiology and DNA suggests that Neanderthals may have been able to produce spoken language. Among other things, the hyoid bone which supports the tongue – an organ vital to articulation – is similar in both species and Neanderthals have a variant of a gene that has been implicated in language called FOXP2, which is very similar to that of humans. So at some point there may have been at least two chattering anthropoids stalking the planet. But why did language evolve? What evolutionary problem existed to which language was the answer. As we shall see, the answer is not clear and may have changed over evolutionary history.

THE EVOLUTIONARY FUNCTION OF LANGUAGE

The problem of trying to find the evolutionary function of language is nicely summed up by neuroanthropologist Terrance Deacon.

> Looking for the adaptive benefits of language is like picking only one dessert in your favorite bakery: there are too many compelling options to choose from. What aspect of human social organisation and adaptation wouldn't benefit from the evolution of language?
>
> (Deacon 1997)

What indeed. One widely discussed benefit of language is that it is designed to 'share ideas', or to 'coordinate action'. But we must be careful that we don't confuse what language can be used for now with what ecological problem(s) language evolved to solve in ancestral times. For example, your remarkably dextrous thumbs can be used to tap out a message on your phone, hitch a lift or signal to someone that everything is OK, but no one would argue the evolution anticipated these very recent uses.

The notion that language might be used to share ideas (or share anything, really) was questioned by a research article by John Krebs and Richard Dawkins (Krebs and Dawkins, 1978) titled 'Animal Signals: Mind Reading and Manipulation'. As that last word suggests, far from seeing animal communication as occurring for mutual benefit or the benefit of the receiver, they proposed that the principal beneficiary is the individual sending the message. Superficially, this seems wrong when we think of many forms of animal communication. Celebrated cases of animal communication such as the dance of the honeybee that informs its hivemates of the location of a nectar source (von Frisch 1955) or the cries uttered by vervet monkeys to warn their group-mates of the presence of a predator (Cheney and Seyfarth 1982) seem to go against this self-centred view of animal communication. However, bees don't really count because they are so highly inter-related (sharing 75 per cent of their genes) that cooperation can be explained by kin-selection (see Chapter 1). As for vervet monkeys, close analysis shows that females are more likely to call when their offspring are threatened compared to unrelated juveniles (and thus protecting their own genetic material – kin selection again) and males are far more likely to call when in the presence of females (with whom they might mate) than other males (Cheney and Seyfarth, 1985).

So in these, and many other cases, communication is tinged with a degree of selfishness (kin selection theory would say that protecting offspring is a selfish act, at the level of the gene, again see Chapter 1).

BOX 7.3 IS LANGUAGE UNIQUE TO HUMANS?

One of the odd things what we humans like to do is to think up reasons as to why we are special. There have been many attempts to come up with reasons for human uniqueness. The philosopher Renee Descartes believed that only humans had a soul, for example. Later, humans were considered to be the only animal that used tools and when other animals were found to use tools, we made the small amendment that we were the only animal that could make tools ('man the toolmaker' we proudly called ourselves). This also fell by the wayside as crows and chimpanzees are now considered to create as opposed to merely use tools, and the list will doubtless grow. For quite some time, language has held firm as a uniquely human endeavour, but is it still a reasonable assumption?

Many animals communicate; we have already discussed vervet monkeys and bees, but neither of these animals has what it takes to be considered a language. Language has many aspects, but one of the most important aspects of human language is our ability to combine words in particular ways to express an infinite number of things and across many domains of experience. Bees' communication is largely limited to the location of a nectar source – they don't use it, as far as we know, to warn of an oncoming storm; vervet monkeys make alarm calls, but do not use it to inform others of the location of food.

Perhaps the best candidate of animal language comes not from chimps or dolphins, as you might expect, but from the prairie dog. This unprepossessing gopher-like animal lives and burrows, as the name suggests, on the American prairie and, thanks to the work of animal behaviourist Con Slobodchikoff, has proven to have remarkable powers of expression. Like vervet monkeys, prairie dogs have a wide range of alarm calls specific to predators such as cayotes and eagles (we might think of them as words) but, more surprisingly, are seemingly capable of generating new words for potential 'predators' that they had never encountered, such as a European ferret or a black oval that Slobodchikoff placed in their territory. Not only were new sounds produced but these sounds were 'understood' by the rest of the community (Slobodchikoff 2002). They also seem to be able to combine individual vocalisations to describe different properties of a threat such as 'red' + 'rectangle'. This is remarkable because so far, no other animal seems to be capable of combining 'words' in this way.

But is this language? Some have argued (Slobodchikoff 2002) that it is, and that those who disagree are guilty of rejecting anything that undermines our linguistic specialness. This may be true, but one way where (so far!) human language differs from prairie dog 'language' is prairie dogs do not use their skills as widely as humans. Humans use their language in all aspects of human endeavour; prairie dogs seem to be largely restricted to alarm calls.

IS HUMAN LANGUAGE ALSO MANIPULATIVE?

To some extent is seems that human language is, indeed, manipulative. Thom Scott-Phillips (2006) suggests that in social situations people frequently compete with each other to be heard, whereas people do not compete with each other to listen. Furthermore, speaking is not conceived of as an altruistic act. On the contrary, talking too much is often seen as selfish, and being a good listener seen as selfless. Finally, if speaking were altruistic with people benefitting from listening, we would expect our anatomy to reflect this, producing ever-more sensitive ears to allow us to eavesdrop and benefit from any pearls of wisdom that might be said, even at a whisper. In fact, it is the opposite. Most of the anatomical changes regarding language have been about language production rather than comprehension (Lieberman 1984), suggesting that the benefit is to speaking rather than listening. For example, a border collie called Rico (Kaminski, Call and Fischer 2004) can respond to over 200 words, but is unable to utter a single one.

Language *can* be selfish. It may have even *begun* as a selfish act as it evolved from more primitive forms of communication but is it now *always* or even *predominantly* a selfish act? The fact that you are reading this book will hopefully suggest to you that it is not. Of course, the authors of books obtain a small remuneration from your purchase, and of course to some extent you might argue that we are trying to manipulate you into our way of thinking, all of which is in accordance with Scott-Phillips' argument, but even if our little book cannot be considered an act of unbridled altruism there is a sense in which it is, at least, mutually beneficial to authors and readers.

As we saw above, chimpanzees may copy each other's actions, but they never seem to directly instruct others, whereas humans – even three-year-olds – will instruct others, whether or not this involves language. So instruction seems to be (so far!) uniquely human and, according to biologist Kevin Laland, language evolved for the purposes of teaching, which speeds up cultural transmission and enables us to copy with greater fidelity. Using language, it is so much easier to give advice on how to behave, directions to the location of food and instructions on how to make useful tools such as axes, baskets, or pots, than if we had to rely on observational learning alone (Laland 2017).

Where does this get us answering the question as to whether language is used for selfish or selfless reasons? The answer probably depends on context. In situations where there is a degree of competition between individuals, language can be used to manipulate others as Krebs and Dawkins and more recently Scott-Phillips have pointed out. But in situations where there is a high degree of mutual interdependency, such as working together to catch prey that will eventually be shared, or in the development of new practices that benefit everyone, language is likely to be used for more selfless means.

SUMMARY

Culture is often perceived of as a force that is separate from biology, but recent evolutionary psychologists have asked the question: what is culture for? One answer is that it enables humans to adapt much more rapidly than by biological evolution in order to respond to changing environmental pressures. This is known as dual inheritance theory. Early attempts to study cultural differences attributed them to biological differences. Things changed when Franz Boas established cultural relativism as a method in social anthropology. This aimed to understand cultural practices within the context of the wider culture. The Boas–Mead view that humans are malleable and cultures infinitely variable has been shown to be incorrect. Brown's work on cultural universals shows a high level of cross-cultural commonality, even though they may differ in detail. Mechanisms such as the ability to imitate are important in order to spread ideas throughout a culture, and humans, it seems, are extremely good imitators. Humans' tendency to conform to authority is also an important motivator for the adoption and spread of cultural practices.

Many modern theories emphasise that culture and biology influenced each other, a process known as gene-culture coevolution and there are examples of instances where cultural practices have selected for specific genotypes, an example being lactose tolerance.

Finally, trade and cultural specialisation have been important in the development of large-scale civilisations, leading to humans' dominance of the planet. One hypothesis suggests our direct ancestor's ability to trade may be one of the reasons why we out-competed Neanderthals.

Language may or may not be uniquely human, but few would deny that human language is far more complex and widely applied than the communications of non-humans. Trying to determine specifically what ecological problems language solves is tricky as it has so many potential benefits. It has been proposed that language, like many instances of non-human communication, might be a selfish act benefitting the sender more than the receiver. But there are also instances where language use can benefit all by speeding up cultural transmission and enabling us to benefit from cultural innovation.

FURTHER READING

Diamond, J. (1998) *Guns, Germs and Steel: A Short History of Everybody for the Last 13,000 Years*. London: Vintage. A really interesting read. Attempts to explain differences in cultural wealth across the planet.

Laland, K. (2017). *Darwin's Unfinished Symphony*. Princeton, NJ: Princeton University Press. Introductory book on the theory of gene culture evolution.

Richerson, P. J. and Boyd, R. (2008) *Not by Genes Alone: How Culture Transformed Human Evolution*. Chicago, IL: University of Chicago Press. Readable book explaining Boyd and Richerson's dual inheritance theory.

GLOSSARY

adaptation Change in populations that arise to solve ancient recurrent challenges.

adenine One of four nucleobases in the DNA molecule which are represented by the letters A, G, C, T. These code for the production of proteins.

affective neuroscience Name given by Jaak Panksepp to an interdisciplinary field of study which combines neuroscience with psychological knowledge of mood emotion and personality.

allele Abbreviation for allelomorph. Every gene occupies a specific location on a chromosome, known as its locus. At any given locus, various forms of a gene may be found. These genes are alleles for that locus.

altruism Self-sacrificing behaviour.

amygdala An almond shaped structure in the forebrain that is involved in processing emotion. A part of the **limbic system**.

Ardipithecus ramidus Early human-like ape (**hominin**) ancestor living in Africa around 4.4 million years ago.

arms race The notion that improvements to one party in competition with another leads to improvements in the other party. In evolution can be applied to predator/prey and host/parasite relationships.

Australopithecus A genus of hominins that appeared in Africa around 4.2 million years ago.

DOI: 10.4324/9780429274428-8

authority ranking Alan Fiske's term for the rules that govern hierarchical relationships.

autism spectrum disorder A developmental disorder that describes a broad spectrum of symptoms including language delay and usually mental retardation. In particular it has been suggested that people with autism have difficulty understanding the mental states of others, i.e. they have an impaired **theory of mind**.

basic emotions Emotional states experienced and expressed that are considered to be found in all cultures. Include fear, rage, happiness, sadness, surprise.

behavioural ecology The study of the evolutionary basis for behaviour in animal species.

behavioural genetics Approach that attempts to separate out the effects on genes and the environment using twin and adoption studies and now new techniques such as genome-wide association studies (GWAS).

behaviourism Approach to psychology most closely associated with B.F. Skinner in which behaviour is studied as the consequence of reinforcements and punishments from the environment.

biparental care The situation where both parents are engaged in providing care for offspring generally including feeding, thermoregulation and protection.

bipedalism The state of walking upright on two legs in contrast to quadrupeds which typically use four limbs for locomotion.

bipolar depression The clinical condition whereby a person oscillates between periods of mania and depression. In most cases there may also be periods of normal mood. Also called bipolar affective disorder.

black box Until recently it was impossible to see inside people's brains and it is still impossible to see inside someone's mind. 'Black box' just refers to this difficulty.

broaden-and-build Barbara Fredrickson's theory that positive emotions can help to expand an individual's cognition and attention.

cheater hypothesis The notion that because most of us engage in broadly prosocial behaviour most of the time, this allows for a small proportion of the population to adopt an alternative free-rider strategy. Has been applied particularly to psychopaths.

chromosome A rod-like body containing a series of genes found in a cell's nucleus.

clinician's illusion The false belief that symptoms are abnormalities rather than traits that are designed to aid recovery

coefficient of relatedness (r) The proportion of genes shared between any two relatives, measured on a scale of 0.0–1.0.

cognitive neuroscience A field of neuroscience which focusses on the biological processes underlying cognition.

community sharing Alan Fiske's term for the rules that govern communities and families.

concordance rates The probability, represented as a percentage, that two related individuals will both have a characteristic.

concordance The correlation between individuals (e.g. **monozygotic** or **dizygotic** twins) on some trait of interest (e.g. intelligence).

concrete operational period Period between seven and 11 years of age in which the child can conserve but has no knowledge of logical relationships.

cooperative breeding Principle where other individuals, relatives but, particularly non-relatives, help with the rearing of children.

cuckoldry The situation where a man is led to believe his wife/partner's offspring is also his, but is in fact the offspring of another man.

cultural relativist school An approach to the social sciences which holds that there are no cultural universals, everything being cultural in origin.

cultural universals Practices that exist in all cultures studied.

cytosine One of four nucleobases in the DNA molecule, which are represented by the letters A, G, C, T. These code for the production of proteins.

Darwinian medicine The application of evolutionary principles to understanding and improving health problems.

deep brain stimulation The procedure that allows for electrical stimulation via an implanted electrode directly to a specific part of the brain.

differential psychology The branch of psychology that examines differences between people in personality and intelligence.

dizygotic twins Non-identical or fraternal twins share 50 per cent of their genes on average (the same as full siblings). The result of two fertilised eggs (di = two, zygote = fertilised egg or ovum).

DNA (deoxyribonucleic acid) A giant double helix molecule that codes for our genes.

dual inheritance theory A theory put forward by Robert Boyd and Peter Richerson that sees culture as a way of transmitting information to enhance fitness (the other route being genetic information).

ecological niche The position of a species within an ecosystem.

environment of evolutionary adaptedness (or adaptation) (EEA) The combination of time, place and ecological pressures faced by a species during its evolution.

episodic memory Memories of experiences, often rich and involving multiple senses.

equality Alan Fiske's term for the morals that govern **equality matching**.

equality matching Alan Fiske's term for the rules that govern reciprocal exchange.

female choice The notion that, because females invest more heavily in the production of offspring, they are more selective than males when it comes to choosing a mate.

fitness The proportion of genes an individual passes on to future generations, either directly via offspring or via aid provided for other relatives such as nephews, nieces and grandchildren.

five factor model The notion that personality can be boiled down to five major traits.

flashbulb memory An unusually detailed memory usually formed as a result of a traumatic (especially collectively traumatic event) such as the death of a famous public figure.

formal operational (or operations) period Period over 11 years of age where the child understands logical relationships (development of formal operations may be dependent on education)

free rider An individual who takes the benefit of reciprocal exchange without paying the cost (sometimes called freeloaders).

frequency dependent selection The process whereby the success of a phenotype (in terms of fitness) depends on the frequency of other phenotypes in a population.

fundamental life tasks Universal human challenges that we see across cultures such as frustrations, losses and accomplishments.

gamete A sperm or egg cell (ova).

gene A section of DNA that codes for one polypeptide. The fundamental unit of heredity.

gene expression The degree to which a gene is active.

gene-culture evolution Approaches to the study of culture which see culture and genes affecting each other.

genome All of an individual's genes.

genotype The genetic constitution of an organism encoded in the nucleus of each cell of the body.

group selection The conception of natural selection as acting at the level of the group.

group socialisation theory A theory proposed by Judith Harris which suggests that peer groups have a greater impact on a child's socialisation and personality development than the parental environment.

group-mindedness Where individuals act with a common goal; people take on the values and practices of the group, rather than acting as individuals.

guanine One of four nucleobases in the DNA molecule which are represented by the letters A, G, C, T. These code for the production of proteins.

heterozygous Having different genes (alleles) at the same position (locus) on each of the paired chromosomes in a cell's nucleus.

hierarchy Alan Fiske's term for the morals that govern **authority ranking**.

hominin Belonging to the human family including current and extinct species.

Homo erectus An ancient ancestor living around 1.8 million to less than 100,000 years ago.

Homo habilis An ancient ancestor living around two million years ago.

Homo sapiens The species to which we all belong. Arose within the last 400,000 years.

homozygous Having identical genes (alleles) at the same position (locus) on each of the paired chromosomes in a cell's nucleus.

Human Genome Project The scheme to identify all of the genes on the human genome.

human non-paternity The technical term for human cuckoldry.

inclusive fitness A measure of the proportion of an individual's genes passing on to future generations directly via offspring and indirectly via other relatives.

incomplete penetrance The condition whereby a gene is not expressed in all individuals that posses it.

indirect reciprocity Principle in which people cooperate with another based on that person's reputation for reciprocating (a way of avoiding **free riders**)

insecure anxious resistant/ambivalent attachment Attachment style in which a person wants to be exceptionally close to another person and is concerned that they will lose them.

insecure avoidant attachment Attachment style in which the individual is relatively non-committal to a relationship.

intersexual selection Competition for members of the opposite sex for the purposes of mating.

intrasexual selection Competition between members of one sex for access to members of the other sex.

kin altruism Self-sacrificing behaviour which provides aid to relatives.

kin selection The part of natural selection where individuals engage in apparently altruistic behaviour in order to favour kin (and help the altruist to pass their genes on indirectly).

locus The location of a specific gene on a chromosome.

major depressive disorder A state of pervasive low mood and lack of energy and motivation.

mania A state of extremely elevated mood.

market pricing Alan Fiske's term for the rules that govern exchange but using money rather than payment in kind as for **equality matching**.

mating mind hypothesis Geoffrey Miller's theory that evolution of the human brain/mind was driven to its current state of complexity largely by sexual selection in order to impress the opposite sex.

Mendel's laws of inheritance The original conception of what later became known as genetics by Austrian Monk Gregor Mendel.

misandry Term used to describe people who dislike, hate or distrust men.

mismatch hypothesis The notion that there is mismatch between our current adaptations which arose during our Pleistocene past and the modern environment.

misogyny Term used to describe people who dislike, hate or distrust women.

Modern Evolutionary Synthesis Term used to describe the combination of Darwinian natural selection and modern genetics (also referred to as Neo-Darwinism).

molecular biology The field which examines the structure and function of DNA and other important biological molecules such as proteins.

monozygotic twins Identical twins sharing 100 per cent of their genes by common decent. All monozygotic twins were once one individual and the result of a single fertilised egg that split into two (mono = one, zygote = the name for a fertilised egg or ovum).

mutation A random inherited change to genetic material.

natural selection The prime mover of evolutionary change. The name given by Darwin to what is today considered to be differential gene replication. May more loosely be described as differential reproductive success of different **phenotypes**.

Neo-Darwinism Term used to describe the combination of Darwinian natural selection and modern genetics (also referred to as Modern Evolutionary Synthesis).

nepotistic strategists Taking care of your close relatives (especially offspring).

neurone A cell that is able to pass on messages by becoming excited or inhibited and which makes up the main components of the nervous system. Also known as nerve cell.

neuroimaging Techniques that enable scientists to observe the operations of brains.

neurotransmitter A chemical released by a neuron in order to communicate with one or more other neurones.

nonshared environment The part of the environment that is unique to one individual. This is particularly used for twin studies; e.g. one twin is bullied, the other is not. Also called the **unique environment**.

normal distribution A bell shaped curve showing the typical distribution of variation in a characteristic such as height or intelligence.

orbitofrontal cortex A portion of the cortex that lies just above the eyes and is involved in processing socially appropriate responses.

over-imitation Where people imitate actions and copy even seemingly irrelevant aspects of the action.

parental investment The effort and resources expended by a parent on each offspring.

parochial altruism Altruistic behaviour focused exclusively on the in-group.

phenotype All of an individual's traits which result from the interaction of genes with the environment.

pleiotropy Where one gene has more than one **phenotypic** effect.

Pleistocene The era that is often referred to as the 'Ice Age' and covers the period from around 2.5 million years ago to around 11,700 years ago.

polyandry The situation where a female of a species mates with more than one male.

polygenic The phenomenon of a trait being coded for by more than one gene.

polygyny The situation where a male of a species mates with more than one female.

polypeptide A relatively simple protein. Some proteins are made up of a single polypeptide, others are made up of more than one.

pre-operational period Period between about two and seven years of age in which the child shows awareness of the object concept, but cannot yet conserve.

proximate level of explanation A level of explanation that considers the immediate causes of a particular trait.

Punnett Square A form of table that summarizes the possible combinations of paternal and maternal genes.

reactive heritability hypothesis The notion that personality characteristics such as extraversion are calibrated during development dependent on other traits. An example of this is an individual who is large and muscular, who might then become more confident and extravert because of the way that others treat them during development.

receptor site A place on the surface of a neurone which receives chemical messages from other neurones and causes the neurone either to increase or decrease its firing rate.

reciprocal altruism Principle developed by Robert Trivers in which cooperation is maintained by reciprocal exchange: 'you scratch my back, and I'll scratch yours'.

Red Queen The hypothesis that adaptations developed by members of one species are counteracted by developments in members of the other species, with particular emphasis on host/parasite relationships.

relational models theory Proposes that there are four elementary mental models: communal sharing, authority ranking, equality matching and market pricing

reproductive value A theoretical measurement of an individual's potential for future production of offspring.

Sahelanthropus tchadensis The earliest known human-like (**hominin**) species believed to date back to around six million years.

schizophrenia A serious psychological disorder where a sufferer may have periods of disordered thought, delusional behaviour, hallucinations and in some cases paranoia.

secure attachment Attachment style in which a person develops typically bonded relationships.

selective advantage A characteristic of an individual which helps boost survival and reproduction in comparison to other members of the population. Is believed to be the basis of Darwinian evolution.

semantic memory Memories of 'facts' that involve little sensory experience. Often abstracted from multiple experiences.

sensorimotor period Period from birth to about two years of age in which Piaget thought the infant develops the object concept (e.g. object permanence).

sexual selection Darwin's other mechanism of evolutionary change. Sexual selection 'selects for' traits which aid an individual in gaining access to mates. Can be divided into intersexual and intrasexual selection.

sexual strategies theory The notion that it is due to different ancient, recurrent reproductive challenges that today we see some differences between the sexes in current psychological make-up.

shared environment The part of the environment that is shared by (e.g. twins). For example the family environment.

sociobiology A framework that attempts to explain social phenomena in terms of biology including genes. There is debate as to whether or not sociobiology is the same thing as evolutionary psychology.

thymine One of four nucleobases in the DNA molecule which are represented by the letters A, G, C, T. These code for the production of proteins.

trait A fundamental characteristic of the **phenotype**.

ultimate level of explanation A level of explanation that attempts to explain the evolutionary function of characteristics including internal states and behaviour.

unique environment See nonshared environment.

unity Alan Fiske's term for the morals that govern **community sharing**.

upward spiral theory A theory of lifestyle change, developed by Barbara Fredrickson and which emphasizes how positive mood can lead to long-term compliance with positive health behaviours.

virtuous violence A concept developed by Alan Fiske to describe people who harm people for what they consider to be 'good' or 'moral' reasons.

zygote A cell that is formed from the fusion of a sperm and an ova (i.e. a fertilised egg).

REFERENCES

Abed, R. and St John-Smith, P. (2022) *Evolutionary Psychiatry: Current Perspectives on Evolution and Mental Health*. Cambridge: Cambridge University Press.

Adelson, E. H. (2000) Lightness perception and lightness illusions. In M. Gazzaniga (Ed.), *The New Cognitive Neurosciences* (2nd edn). Cambridge, MA: MIT Press, pp. 339–335.

Adler, A. (1928) Characteristics of the first, second, and third child. *Children*, 3, 14–52.

Anderson, K. (2006) How well does paternity confidence match actual paternity? Evidence from worldwide nonpaternity rates. *Current Anthropology*, 47(3), 513–520.

Andersson, M. (1982) Female choice selects for extreme tail length in a widowbird. *Nature*, 299, 818–820.

Andreoni, J. and Miller, J. (1993) Rational cooperation in the finitely repeated prisoner's dilemma: Experimental evidence. *The Economic Journal*, 103, 570–585.

Andrew, R. J. (1963a) The origins and evolution of the calls and facial expressions of the primates. *Behaviour*, 20, 1–109.

Andrew, R. J. (1963b) Evolution of facial expressions. *Science*, 142, 1034–1041.

Archer, J. (2019) The reality and evolutionary significance of human psychological sex differences. *Biological Review*, 94, 1381–1415.

Armon-Jones, C. (1985) Prescription, explication and the social construction of emotion. *Journal for the Theory of Social Behaviour*, 15, 1–22.

Asch, S. E. (1951) Effects of group pressure upon the modification and distortion of judgments. *Groups, Leadership, and Men*, 222–236.

Auyeung, B., Baron-Cohen, S., Chapman, E., Knickmeyer, R., Taylor, K. and Hackett, G. (2009) Foetal testosterone and autistic traits. *British Journal of Psychology*, 100, 1–22.

Auyeung, B., Taylor, K., Hackett, G., and Baron-Cohen, S. (2010) Fetal testosterone and autistic traits in 18 to 24-month-old children, *Molecular Autism*, 1, 11.

Babiak, P., and Hare, R. D. (2006) *Snakes in Suits: When Psychopaths Go to Work*. New York, NY: Regan Books/Harper Collins.

Babiak, P. and Hare, R. D. (2019) *Snakes in Suits: Understanding and Surviving the Psychopaths in Your Office* (Rev edn). New York, NY: HarperCollins.

Baillargeon, R. (1987) Object permanence in 3½-and 4½-month-old infants. *Developmental psychology*, 23(5), 655.

Baker, R. R. and Bellis, M. A. (1995) *Human Sperm Competition: Copulation Masturbation, and Infidelity*. London: Chapman & Hall.

Barkow, J. H. (1989) *Darwin, Sex, and Status: Biological Approaches to Mind and Culture*. Toronto: University of Toronto.

Barkow, J. H. (Ed.). (2006) *Missing the Revolution: Darwinism for Social Scientists*. Oxford: Oxford University Press.

Barkow, J. H., Cosmides, L. and Tooby, J. (Eds.) (1992) *The Adapted Mind: Evolutionary Psychology and the Generation of Culture*. Oxford/New York: Oxford University Press.

Barrett, L. F. (2013) Psychological Construction: The Darwinian Approach to the Science of Emotion. *Emotion Review*, 5, 379–389.

Barrett, L. F. (2018) *How Emotions are Made: The Secret Life of the Brain*. Boston, MA: Mariner Books.

Bateson, P., Mendl, M., and Feaver, J. (1990) Play in the domestic cat is enhanced by rationing of the mother during lactation. *Animal Behaviour*, 40 (3), 514–525.

Belsky, J. (1999) Modern evolutionary theory and patterns of attachment. In J. Cassidy and P. R. Shaver (Eds.), *Handbook of Attachment: Theory, Research, and Clinical Applications*New York, NY: The Guilford Press, pp. 141–161.

Belsky, J., Houts, R. M., and Fearon, R. P. (2010) Infant attachment security and the timing of puberty testing an evolutionary hypothesis. *Psychological Science*, 21(9), 1195–1201.

Belsky, J., Steinberg, L. D., Houts, R. M., Friedman, S. L., DeHart, G., Cauffman, E., … and NICHD Early ChildCare Research Network. (2007) Family rearing antecedents of pubertal timing. *Child development*, 78(4), 1302–1321.

Bernhard, H., Fischbacher, U. and Fehr, E. (2006) Parochial altruism in humans. *Nature*, 442(7105), 912–915.

Betzig, L. (1986) *Despotism and Differential Reproduction: A Darwinian View of History*. Hawthorne, NY: Aldine de Gruyter.

Billig, M. (2002) Henri Tajfel's 'Cognitive aspects of prejudice'and the psychology of bigotry. *British Journal of Social Psychology*, 41(2), 171–188.

Bloom, G., and Sherman, P. W. (2005) Dairying barriers affect the distribution of lactose malabsorption. *Evolution and Human Behavior*, 26(4), 301–312.

Bowlby, J. (1969) *Attachment and Loss*. New York, NY: Basic Books.
Bowles, S. and Gintis, H. (2000) Reciprocity, self-interest, and the welfare state. *Nordic Journal of Political Economy,* 26(1), 33–53.
Boyd, R., Richerson, P. J. and Henrich, J. (2011) Rapid cultural adaptation can facilitate the evolution of large-scale cooperation. *Behavioral Ecology and Sociobiology*, 65, 431–444.
Brown, D. E. (1991) *Human Universals*. New York, NY: McGraw-Hill.
Brown, R. and Kulik, J. (1977) Flashbulb memories. *Cognition*, 5(1), 73–99.
Buller, D.J. (2005) Evolutionary psychology: The emperor's new paradigm. *Trends in Cognitive Science*, 9, 277–283.
Burns, J. (2007) *The Descent of Madness: Evolutionary Origins of Psychosis and the Social Brain*. New York, NY: Routledge.
Burnstein, E., Crandell, C. and Kitayama, S. (1994) Some neo-Darwinian decision rules for altruism: Weighing cues for inclusive fitness as a function of the biological importance of the decision. *Journal of Personality and Social Psychology*, 67, 773–789.
Buss, D. M. (1989) Sex differences in human mate preferences: Evolutionary hypotheses tested in 37 cultures. *Behavioral and Brain Sciences*, 12, 1–49.
Buss, D. M. (2016) *The Evolution of Desire: Strategies of Human Mating*. New York, NY: Basic Books.
Buss, D. M. (2019) *Evolutionary Psychology: The New Science of the Mind* (6th edn). New York, NY: Routledge.
Buss, D. M. and Hawley, P. (Eds.) (2011) *The Evolution of Personality and Individual Differences*. Oxford: Oxford University Press.
Buss, D. M. and Schmitt, D. P. (1993) Sexual strategies theory: An evolutionary perspective on human mating. *Psychological Review*, 100, 204–232.
Buss, D. M. and Schmidt, D. P. (2019) Mate preferences and their behavioral manifestations. *Annual Review of Psychology*, 70, 77–110.
Buss, D. M., Larsen, R. J., Westen, D., and Semmelroth, J. (1992) Sex differences in jealousy: Evolution, physiology, and psychology. *Psychological Science*, 3, 251–255.
Bussey, K. and Bandura, A. (1999) Social cognitive theory of gender development and differentiation. *Psychological Review*, 106, 676–713.
Carter, R. T. and Qureshi, A. (1995) A typology of philosophical assumptions in multi-cultural counseling and training. In J. G. Ponterotto, J. M. Casas, L. A. Suzuki and C. M. Alexander (Eds.), *Handbook of Multicultural Counseling*. Thousand Oaks, CA: Sage, pp. 239–262.
Catchpole, C. K. and Slater, P. J. B. (2008) *Bird Song: Biological Themes and Variations*. Cambridge: Cambridge University Press.
Cattell, R. B. (1965) *The Scientific Analysis of Personality*. Chicago, IL: Aldine.
Chang, L., Lu, H. J., Lansford, J. E., Skinner, A. T., Bornstein, M. H., Steinberg, L., … and Tapanya, S. (2019) Environmental harshness and

unpredictability, life history, and social and academic behavior of adolescents in nine countries. *Developmental Psychology*, 55(4), 890.

Cheney, D. L. and Seyfarth, R. M. (1982) How vervet monkeys perceive their grunts: Field playback experiments. *Animal Behaviour*, 30(3), 739–751.

Cheney, D. L. and Seyfarth, R. M. (1985) Vervet monkey alarm calls: Manipulation through shared information? *Behaviour*, 94(1–2), 150–166.

Choi, J. H. and Yoo, H. W. (2013) Control of puberty: genetics, endocrinology, and environment. *Current Opinion in Endocrinology: Diabetes and Obesity*, 20(1), 62–68.

Clutton-Brock, T. H. (2009) Cooperation between non-kin in animal societies. *Nature*, 462, 51–57.

Clutton-Brock, T. and McAuliffe, K. (2009) Female mate choice in mammals. *Quarterly Review of Biology*, 84, 3–27.

Colquhoun, L., Workman and Fowler, J. (2020) The problem of altruism and future directions. In L. Workman, R. Reader and J. H. Barkow (Eds.), *Cambridge Handbook of Evolutionary Perspectives on Human Behavior*. Cambridge: Cambridge University Press.

Conleyn, B. A. (2020) Mayr and Tinbergen: Disentangling and integrating. *Biology and Philosophy*, 35(4). https://doi.org/10.1007/s10539-019-9731-x.

Cosmides, L. and Tooby, J. (1992) Cognitive adaptations for social exchange. In J. Barkow, L. Cosmides and J. Tooby (Eds.), *The Adapted Mind*. New York, NY: Oxford University Press, pp. 163–228.

Craddock, N., O'Donovan, M. C. and Owen, M. J. (2005) The genetics of schizophrenia and bipolar disorder: dissecting psychosis. *Journal of Medical Genetics*, 42:193–204.

Curry, O. S. (2016) Morality as cooperation: A problem-centred approach. In T. K. Shackelford and R. D. Hansen (Eds.) *The Evolution of Morality*. Cham: Springer, pp. 27–51.

Curry, O. S., Mullins, D. A. and Whitehouse, H. (2019) Is it good to cooperate? Testing the theory of morality-as-cooperation in 60 societies. *Current Anthropology*, 60(1), 47–69.

Daly, M. and Wilson, M. (1983) *Sex, Evolution and Behaviour* (2nd edn). Belmont, CA: Wadsworth.

Daly, M. and Wilson, M. (1998) *The truth about Cinderella: A Darwinian view of parental love*. New Haven, CT: Yale University Press.

Daly, M. and Wilson, M. (2005) The 'Cinderella effect' is no fairy tale. *Trends in Cognitive Sciences*, 9, 507–508.

Daly, M. and Wilson, M. (2007) Is the 'Cinderella Effect' controversial? In C. B. Crawford and D. L. Krebs (Eds.), *Foundations of Evolutionary Psychology*. Mahwah, NJ: Erlbaum, pp. 383–400.

Darwin, C. (1859) *On the Origin of Species by Natural Selection*. London: Murray.

Darwin, C. (1871) *The Descent of Man, and Selection in Relation to Sex*. London: Murray.

Darwin, C. (1872) *The Expression of the Emotions in Man and Animals*. London: HarperCollins.

Dawkins, R. (1976) *The Selfish Gene* (1st edn). Oxford: Oxford University Press.

de Waal, F. B. M. (2003) Darwin's legacy and the study of primate visual communication. In P. Ekman, J. J. Campos, R. J. Davidson and F. B. M. de Waal (Eds.), *Emotions Inside Out: 130 Years After Darwin's The Expression of the Emotions in Man and Animals* (*Annals of the New York Academy of Sciences*, 1000, pp. 7–31). New York, NY: New York Academy of Sciences.

Degler, C. N. (1991) *In Search of Human Nature: The Decline and Revival of Darwinism in American Social Thought*. New York, NY: Oxford University Press.

Diamond, J. (1998) *Guns, Germs and Steel: A Short History of Everybody for the Last 13,000 Years*. London: Vintage.

Dingemanse, N. J., Both, C., Drent, P. J., and Tinbergen, J. M. (2004) Fitness consequences of avian personalities in a fluctuating environment. *Proceedings of the Royal Society of London, Series B: Biological Sciences*, 271(1541), 847–852.

Dobzhansky, T. (1973) Nothing in biology makes sense except in the light of evolution. *American Biology Teacher*, 35, 125–129.

Duckworth, R. A. (2010) Evolution of personality: Developmental constraints on behavioural flexibility. *Auk*, 127, 752–758.

Dudley, R. (2002) Fermenting fruit and the historical ecology of ethanol ingestion: is alcoholism in modern humans an evolutionary hangover? *Addiction*, 97, 381–388.

Dunbar, R. I. M. (2014) *Human Evolution: A Pelican Introduction*. London: Pelican.

Dunbar, R. I. M. (2021) *Friends: Understanding the Power of our Most Important Relationships*. London: Watson Little.

Dunbar, R. I. M., Clark, A. and Hurst, N. L. (1995) Conflict and cooperation among the Vikings: Contingent behavioural decisions. *Ethology and. Sociobiology*, 16, 233–246.

Eibl-Eibesfeldt, I. (1973) *Social Communication and Movement*. New York, NY: Academic Press.

Ekman, P. (1999) Basic emotions. In T. Dalgleish and M. Power (Eds), *Handbook of Cognition and Emotion, Facial Expressions*. New York: John Wiley & Sons, pp. 45–60.

Ekman, P. (2009) Darwin's contributions to our understanding of emotional expressions. *Philosophical Transactions of the Royal Society of London – Series B: Biological Sciences*, 36, 3449–3451.

Ekman, P. and Cordaro, D. (2011) What is meant by calling emotions basic ? *Emotion Review*, 3, 364–370.

Ekman, P. and Friesen, W. V. (1971) Constants across cultures in the face and emotion. *Journal of Personality and Social Psychology*, 17, 124–129.

Emlen, S. T. and Wrege, P. H. (2004) Division of labour in parental care behaviour of a sex-role-reversed shorebird, the wattled jacana. *Animal Behaviour*, 68, 847–855.

Emlen, S. T. and Wrege, P. H. (2004) Size dimorphism, intrasexual competition, and sexual selection in wattled jacana (Jacana jacana), a sex-role-reversed shorebird in Panama. *The Auk*, 121(2), 391–403.

Eysenck, H. J. and Eysenck, S.B.G. (1976) *Psychoticism as a Dimension of Personality*. New York, NY: Crane, Russak, & Company.

Fagen, R. M. (1977) Selection for optimal age-dependent schedules of play behavior. *American Naturalist*, 111, 395–414.

Fehr, E. and Gächter, S. (2000) Fairness and retaliation: The economics of reciprocity. *Journal of Economic Perspectives*, 14, 159–181.

Fehr, E. and Schmidt, K. M. (1999) A theory of fairness, competition, and cooperation. *The Quarterly Journal of Economics*, 114(3), 817–868.

Fiske, A. P. and Rai, T. S. (2014) *Virtuous Violence: Hurting and Killing to Create, Sustain, End, and Honor Social Relationships*. Cambridge: Cambridge University Press.

Fowler, J. H., Baker, L. A. and Dawes, C. T. (2008) Genetic variation in political participation. *American Political Science Review*, 102(2), 233–248.

Frank, R. H. (1988) *Passions within Reason: The Strategic Role of the Emotions*. New York, NY: W.W. Norton and Company.

Fredrickson, B. L. (1998) What good are positive emotions? *Review of General Psychology*, 2, 300–319.

Fredrickson, B. L. (2013) Positive emotions broaden and build. *Advances in Experimental Social Psychology*, 47, 1–53.

Fredrickson, B. L. (2013) Positive emotions broaden and build. In E. Ashby Plant and P. G. Devine (Eds.), *Advances on Experimental Social Psychology*. Burlington, IN: Academic Press, pp. 1–53.

Fredrickson, B. L. and Joiner, T. (2018) Reflections on positive emotions and upward spirals. *Perspectives on Psychological Science*, 13(2), 194–199.

Furnham, A. and Cheng, H. (2015) The stability and change of malaise scores over 27 years: Findings from a nationally representative sample. *Personality and Individual Differences*, 79, 30–34.

Furnham, A. and Kanazawa, S. (2020) The evolution of personality. In L. Workman, W. Reader and J. H. Barkow (Eds.), *The Cambridge Handbook of Evolutionary Perspectives on Human Behavior*. Cambridge: Cambridge University Press, pp. 462–470.

Gamble, C. (1999) *The Palaeolithic Societies of Europe*. Cambridge: Cambridge University Press.

Gardner, H. W. (2006) *Multiple Intelligences: New Horizons*. New York, NY: Basic Books.

Gardner, H. W. (2010) A debate on "multiple intelligences". In J. Traub (Ed.), *Cerebrum: Forging Ideas in Brain Science*. Washington, DC: Dana Press, pp. 34–61.

Geary, D. C., Vigil, J. and Byrd-Craven, J. (2004) Evolution of human mate choice. *Journal of Sexuality Research*, 41, 27–42.

Gershon, E. S., Martinez, M., Goldin, L. R. and Gejman, P. V. (1990) Genetic mapping of common diseases: The challenges of manic-depressive illness and schizophrenia. *Trends in Genetics*, 6, 282–287.

Ghiselin, M. T. (1973) Darwin and evolutionary psychology: Darwin initiated a radically new way of studying behavior. *Science*, 179(4077), 964–968.

Gigerenzer, G. (1991) How to make cognitive illusions disappear: Beyond 'heuristics and biases'. *European Review of Social Psychology*, 2(1), 83–115.

Gintis, H. (2007) A framework for the unification of the behavioral sciences. *Behavioral and Brain Sciences*, 30(1), 1–16.

Glick, P. and Fiske, S. T. (1997) Hostile and benevolent sexism: Measuring ambivalent sexist attitudes toward women. *Psychology of Women Quarterly*, 21, 119–135.

Gluckman, P., Beedle, A. Buklijas, T., Low, F. and Hanson, M. (2016) *Principles of Evolutionary Medicine* (2nd edn). Oxford: Oxford University Press.

Gopnik, A., Meltzoff, A. N. and Kuhl, P. K. (2001) *How Babies Think: The Science of Childhood*. London: Phoenix.

Griggs, R. A. and Cox, J. R. (1982) The elusive thematic-materials effect in Wason's selection task. *British Journal of Psychology*, 73(3), 407–420.

Hallmayer, J., Cleveland, S., Torres, A., Phillips, J., Cohen, B., Torigoe, T., … and Risch, N. (2011) Genetic heritability and shared environmental factors among twin pairs with autism. *Archives of General Psychiatry*, 68(11), 1095–1102.

Hamann, K., Warneken, F., Greenberg, J. R. and Tomasello, M. (2011) Collaboration encourages equal sharing in children but not in chimpanzees. *Nature*, 476(7360), 328–331.

Hamilton, W. D. (1964a and 1964b) The genetical evolution of social behaviour (vols I and II). *Journal of Theoretical Biology*, 7, 1–52.

Hamilton, W. D., Axelrod, R. and Tanese, R. (1990) Sexual reproduction as an adaptation to resist parasites. *Proceedings of the National Academy of Science USA*, 87, 3566–3573.

Harris, J. R. (1998) *The Nurture Assumption: Why Children Turn Out the Way They Do*. New York, NY: Simon & Schuster.

Harris, J. R. (2009) *The Nurture Assumption: Why Children Turn Out the Way They Do* (2nd edn). London: Simon & Schuster.

Harris, J. R. and Workman, L. (2016) When life hands you a lemon, just bite in. Judith Rich Harris takes Lance Workman through her extraordinary fight back against entrenched views of child development. *The Psychologist*, 29, 696–697.

Hidaka, B. H. (2012) Depression as a disease of modernity: explanations for increasing prevalence. *Journal of Affective Disorders*, 140, 205–214.

Hill, R. A. and Barton, R. A. (2005) Red enhances human performance in contests. *Nature*, 435(7040), 293.

Hoebel, E. A. (1966) *Anthropology: The Study of Man*. New York, NY: McGraw-Hill.

Horan, R. D., Bulte, E., and Shogren, J. F. (2005) How trade saved humanity from biological exclusion: An economic theory of Neanderthal extinction. *Journal of Economic Behavior and Organization*, 58(1), 1–29.

Hrdy, S. B. (2009) *Mothers and Others: The Evolutionary Origins of Mutual Understanding*. Cambridge, MA: Harvard University Press.

Hrdy, S. B. (2017) Comes the child before man: How cooperative breeding and prolonged postweaning dependence shaped human potential. In *Hunter-Gatherer Childhoods*. London: Routledge, pp. 65–91.

Humphrey, L. and Stringer, C. (2019) *Our Human Story*. London: Natural History Museum.

Hyde, J. S. (2014) Gender similarities and differences. *Annual Review of Psychology*, 65, 373–398.

Ilardi, S. S. (2010) *The Depression Cure: The 6-Step Program to Beat Depression without Drugs*. Cambridge, MA: Da Capo Press.

Ilardi, S. S., Jacobson, J. D., Lehman, K. A., Stites, B. A., Karwoski, L., Stroupe, N. N. and Young, C. (2007) *Therapeutic lifestyle change for depression: Results from a randomized controlled trial*. Paper presented at the Annual Meeting of the Association for Behavioral and Cognitive Therapy, Philadelphia, PA.

Ingram, C. M., Troendle, N. J., Gill, C. A., Braude, S. and Honeycutt, R. L. (2015) Challenging the inbreeding hypothesis in a eusocial mammal: population genetics of the naked mole-rat, *Heterocephalus glaber*. *Molecular Ecology*, 24(19), 4848–4865.

James, W. (1884) What is an emotion? *Mind*, 9, 188–205.

Jamison, K. R. (1993) *Touched with Fire: Manic-Depressive Illness and the Artistic Temperament*. New York, NY: The Free Press.

Jamison, K. R. (2011) Great wits and madness: More near allied? *British Journal of Psychiatry*, 199, 351–352.

Kaminski, J., Call, J. and Fischer, J. (2004) Word learning in a domestic dog: Evidence for 'fast mapping'. *Science*, 304(5677), 1682–1683.

Kawai, M. (1965) Newly-acquired pre-cultural behavior of the natural troop of Japanese monkeys on Koshima Islet. *Primates*, 6(1), 1–30.

Keller, M. C. and Nesse, R. M. (2006) The evolutionary significance of depressive symptoms: Different adverse situations lead to different depressive symptom patterns. *Journal of Personality and Social Psychology*, 91, 316–330.

Kellogg, W. N. and Kellogg, L. A. (1933) *The Ape and the Child: A Study of Environmental Influence upon Early Behavior*. New York NY: McGraw-Hill.

Koch, H. (1955) Some personality correlates of sex, sibling position, and sex of sibling among five- and six-year-old children. *Genetic Psychology Monographs*, 52, 3–50.

Koch, H. (1956) Attitudes of young children toward their peers as related to certain characteristics of their siblings. *Psychological Monographs*, 70, 1–41.

Krebs, J. R. and Dawkins, R. (1978) Animal signals: Mind-reading and manipulation. In J. R. Krebs and N. B. Davies (Eds.), *Behavioural Ecology: An Evolutionary Approach*. Oxford: Blackwell, pp. 380–402.

Krieger, F., Becker, N., Greiff, S., and Spinath, F. M. (2019) Big-Five personality and political orientation: Results from four panel studies with representative German samples. *Journal of Research in Personality*, 80, 78–83.

Kring, A. M. and Johnson, S. L. (2019) *Abnormal Psychology; The Science and Treatment of Psychological Disorders* (14th edn). New York, NY: John Wiley & Sons.

Kruger, D. J. and Nesse, R. M. (2006) An evolutionary life-history framework for understanding sex differences in human mortality rates. *Human Nature*, 17, 74–97.

Kuhl, P. K., Williams, K. A., Lacerda, F., Stevens, K. N. and Lindblom, B. (1992) Linguistic experience alters phonetic perception in infants by 6 months of age. *Science*, 255(5044), 606–608.

Kuzawa, C. W., Chugani, H. T., Grossman, L. I., Lipovich, L., Muzik, O., Hof, P. R., … and Lange, N. (2014) Metabolic costs and evolutionary implications of human brain development. *Proceedings of the National Academy of Sciences*, 111(36), 13010–13015.

Lai, M., Lombardo, M., Chakrabarti, B., Ecker, C., Sadek, S., Wheelwright, S., Murphy, D., Suckling, J., Bullmore, E., MRC AIMS Consortium and Baron-Cohen, S. (2012) Individual differences in brain structure underpin empathizing-systemizing cognitive styles in male adults. *NeuroImage*, 61, 1347–1354.

Laland, K. (2017) *Darwin's Unfinished Symphony*. Princeton, NJ: Princeton University Press.

LeDoux, J. E. (2012) Evolution of human emotion: A view through fear. *Progress in Brain Research*, 195, 431–442.

Lee, R. B. (1979) *The Kung San: Men, Women and Work in Foraging Society*. Cambridge: Cambridge University Press.

Lewontin, R. (1970) Race and intelligence. *Bulletin of the Atomic Scientists*, 26(3), 2–8.

Lieberman, P. (1984) *The Biology and Evolution of Language*. Cambridge, MA: Harvard University Press.

Lukaszewski, A. W. and Roney, J. R. (2011) The origins of extraversion: Joint effects of facultative calibration and genetic polymorphism. *Personality and Social Psychology*, 37(3), 409.

Lukaszewski, A. W. and von Rueden, C. (2015) The extraversion continuum in evolutionary perspective: A review of recent theory and evidence. *Personality and Individual Differences*, 77, 186–192.

Lyons, D. E., Young, A. G. and Keil, F. C. (2007) The hidden structure of overimitation. *Proceedings of the National Academy of Sciences*, 104(50), 19751–19756.

Madsen, E. A., Tunney, R. J., Fieldman, G., Plotkin, H. C., Dunbar, R. I., Richardson, J. M., and McFarland, D. (2007) Kinship and altruism: A cross-cultural experimental study. *British Journal of Psychology*, 98(2), 339–359.

Manktelow, K. I. and Evans, J. S. B. (1979) Facilitation of reasoning by realism: Effect or non-effect? *British Journal of Psychology*, 70(4), 477–488.

Marlowe, F. W. (2003) A critical period for provisioning by Hadza men: Implications for pair bonding. *Evolution and Human Behavior*, 24, 217–229.

Marr, D. (1982) *Vision: A Computational Investigation into the Human Representation and Processing of Visual Information*. New York, NY: Henry Holt.

Martin, R. D. (1990) *Primate Origins and Evolution*. London: Chapman & Hall.

Maynard Smith, J. (1978) *The Evolution of Sex*. Cambridge: Cambridge University Press.

Mayr, E. (1961) Cause and effect in biology. *Science*, 134, 1501–1506.

McCrae, R. R. and Costa, P. T., Jr. (1987) Validation of the five-factor model of personality across instruments and observers. *Journal of Personality and Social Psychology*, 52, 81–90.

Mealey, L. (1995) The sociobiology of sociopathy: An integrated evolutionary model. *Behavioral and Brain Sciences*, 18(3), 523–541.

Miller, G. F. (2000) *The Mating Mind: How Sexual Choice Shaped the Evolution of Human Nature*. London: Heinemann/Doubleday.

Moalem, S. (2020) *The Better Half: On the Genetic Superiority of Women*. London: Allen Lane.

Moon, C., Lagercrantz, H. and Kuhl, P. K. (2013) Language experienced in utero affects vowel perception after birth: A two-country study. *Acta Paediatrica*, 102(2), 156–160.

Morton, J. and Johnson, M. H. (1991) CONSPEC and CONLERN: a two-process theory of infant face recognition. *Psychological Review*, 98(2), 164.

Mottron, L. (2011) Changing perceptions: The power of autism. *Nature*, 479, 33–35.

Nagell, K., Olguin, R. S. and Tomasello, M. (1993) Processes of social learning in the tool use of chimpanzees – *Pan troglodytes* – and human children – *Homo sapiens*. *Journal of Comparative Psychology*, 107(2), 174.

Nairne, J. S., and Pandeirada, J. N. (2008) Adaptive memory: Is survival processing special? *Journal of Memory and Language*, 59(3), 377–385.

Nesse, R. M. (2005) Natural selection and the regulation of defenses: a signal detection analysis of the smoke detector principle. *Evolution and Human Behavior*, 26, 88–105.

Nesse, R. M. (2019) *Good Reasons for Feeling Bad: Insights from the Frontier of Evolutionary Psychiatry*. London: Allen Lane.

Nettle, D. (2005) An evolutionary perspective on the extraversion continuum. *Evolution and Human Behavior*, 26, 363–373.

Nettle, D. (2006) The evolution of personality variation in humans and other animals. *American Psychologist*, 61, 622–631.

Nettle, D. and Frankenhuis, W. E. (2020) Life-history theory in psychology and evolutionary biology: one research programme or two?. *Philosophical Transactions of the Royal Society B*, 375(1803).

Nettle, D., Coall, D. A. and Dickins, T. E. (2011) Early-life conditions and age at first pregnancy in British women. *Proceedings of the Royal Society, B*, 278, 1721–1727.

Neuberg, S. L., Kenrick, D. T. and Schaller, M. (2010) Evolutionary social psychology. In S. T. Fiske, D. Gilbert and G. Lindzey (Eds.), *Handbook of Social Psychology* (5th edn). New York, NY: John Wiley & Sons, pp. 761–796.

Nowak, M. A. (2006) Five rules for the evolution of cooperation. *Science*, 314 (5805), 1560–1563.

Nowak, M. A., and Sigmund, K. (2005) Evolution of indirect reciprocity. *Nature*, 437(7063), 1291–1298.

Pallen, M. (2009) *The Rough Guide to Evolution*. Penguin: London.

Panksepp, J. (1998) *Affective Neuroscience: The Foundations of Human and Animal Emotions*. New York, NY: Oxford University Press.

Panksepp, J., and Davis, K. (2018) *The Emotional Foundations of Personality: A Neurobiological and Evolutionary Approach*. New York, NY: W.W. Norton and Company.

Passingham, R. (2016) *Cognitive Neuroscience: A Very Short Introduction*. Oxford: Oxford University Press.

Pawlowki, B., Dunbar, R. I. M. and Lipowicz, A. (2000) Tall men have more reproductive success. *Nature*, 403, 156.

Pinker, S. (1997) *How the Mind Works*. New York, NY: W.W. Norton & Co.

Plomin, R. (2018) *Blueprint: How DNA Makes Us Who We Are*. London: Allen Lane/Penguin Books.

Plomin, R. (2019) *Blueprint, with a New Afterword: How DNA Makes Us Who We Are*. Cambridge, MA: MIT Press.

Plomin, R. and Daniels, D. (1987) Why are children in the same family so different from one another? *Behavioral and Brain Sciences*, 10(1), 1–16.

Plomin, R., DeFries, J. C., Knopik, V. S. and Neiderhiser, J. M. (2012) *Behavioral Genetics* (6th edn). New York, NY: Worth Publishers.

Price, M. E., Cosmides, L. and Tooby, J. (2002) Punitive sentiment as an anti-free rider psychological device. *Evolution and Human Behavior*, 23(3), 203–231.

Ray, W. J. (2013) *Evolutionary Psychology: Neuroscience Perspectives Concerning Human Behavior and Experience*. Thousand Oaks, CA: Sage.

Ray, W. J. (2018) *Abnormal Psychology: Neuroscience Determinants of Human Behavior And Experience* (2nd edn). Thousand Oaks, CA: Sage.

Read, L. E. (1958) *I, Pencil*. Irvington-on-Hudson, NY: Foundation for Economic Education.

Reader, W. and Hughes, S. (2020) The evolution and function of third-party moral judgment. In L. Workman, W. R. Reader and J. H. Barkow (Eds.). *The Cambridge Handbook of Evolutionary Perspectives on Human Behavior*. Cambridge: Cambridge University Press.

Rebers, S. and Koopmans, R. (2012) Altruistic punishment and between-group competition: evidence from n-person prisoner's dilemmas. *Human Nature*, 23, 173–190.

Richards, R. J. (1986) A defense of evolutionary ethics. *Biology and Philosophy*, 1(3), 265–293.

Richerson, P. J. and Boyd, R. (2008) *Not by Genes Alone: How Culture Transformed Human Evolution*. Chicago, IL: University of Chicago Press.

Ridley, M. (1993) *The Red Queen: Sex and the Evolution of Human Nature*. London: Penguin.

Ridley, M. (1996) *The Origins of Virtue*. London: Viking Press.

Ridley, M. (2010) When ideas have sex. TedGlobal [video file] retrieved May, 2014 from www.ted.com/talks/matt_ridley_when_ideas_have_sex.

Sapolsky, R. M. (2018) *Behave: The Biology of Humans at Our Best and Worst*. New York, NY: Penguin.

Schacter, D. L. (2001) *The Seven Sins of Memory*. New York, NY: Houghton Mifflin.

Schaller, M., Simpson, J. A. and Kenrick, D. T. (2006) *Evolution and Social Psychology: Frontiers of Social Psychology*. New York, NY: Psychology Press.

Scott-Phillips, T. C. (2006) *Why talk? Speaking as selfish behaviour*. In A. Cangelosi, et al. (Eds.), The Evolution of Language: Proceedings of the 6th

International Conference on the Evolution of Language. Singapore: World Scientific, pp. 299–306.

Segerstråle, U. (2000) *Defenders of the Truth: The Sociobiology Debate*. Oxford: Oxford University Press.

Shahack-Gross, R., Berna, F., Karkanas, P., Lemorini, C., Gopher, A. and Barkai, R. (2014) Evidence for the repeated use of a central hearth at Middle Pleistocene (300 ky ago) Qesem Cave, Israel. *Journal of Archaeological Science*, 44, 12–21.

Shaver, P. and Hazan, C. (1987) Being lonely, falling in love. *Journal of Social Behavior and Personality*, 2(2), 105.

Skalkos, Z. M. G., Van Dyke, J. U., Camilla, M. and Whittington, C. M. (2020) Paternal nutrient provisioning during male pregnancy in the seahorse *Hippocampus abdominalis*. *Journal of Comparative Physiology B*, 190, 547–556.

Slobodchikoff, C. N. (2002) Cognition and communication in prairie dogs. In M. Bekoff, C. Allen and G. Burghardt (Eds.), *The Cognitive Animal*. Cambridge, MA: MIT Press, pp. 257–264.

Soliman, A., De Sanctis, V. and Elalaily, R. (2014) Nutrition and pubertal development. *Indian Journal of Endocrinology and Metabolism*, 18, S39–S47. https://doi.org/10.4103/2230–8210.145073.

Somers, J. M., Goldner, E.M., Waraich, P. and Hsu, L. (2006) Prevalence and incidence studies of anxiety disorders: a systematic review of the literature. *Canadian Journal of Psychiatry* 51, 100–113.

Spelke, E. S., Breinlinger, K., Macomber, J., and Jacobson, K. (1992) Origins of knowledge. *Psychological Review*, 99(4), 605.

Srinivasan, S., Bettella, F., Mattingsdal, M., Wang, Y., Witoelar, A., Schork, A. J., Thompson, W. K., Zuber, V., Winsvold, B. S., et al. (2016) Genetic markers of human evolution are enriched in schizophrenia. *Biological Psychiatry*, 80(4), 284–292.

Sternberg, R. J. (2021) *Adaptive Intelligence: Surviving and Thriving in Times of Uncertainty*. Cambridge: Cambridge University Press.

Stewart-Williams, S., Chang, C. Y. M., Wong, X. L., Jesse, D., Blackburn, D. and Thomas. A. G. (2021) Reactions to male-favoring vs. female-favoring sex differences: A pre-registered experiment and Southeast Asian replication. *British Journal of Psychology*, 112, 389–411.

Stewart-Williams, S., Wong, X. L, Chang, C. Y. M. and Thomas, A. G. (2022) People react more positively to female- than to male-favoring sex differences: A direct replication of a counterintuitive finding. *PLoS ONE*, 17(3), e0266171.

Stock, J. T. (2008) Are humans still evolving? *EMBO Reports*, 9, 51–54.

Stulp, G., Buunk, A. P. and Pollet, T. V. (2013) Women want taller men more than men want shorter women. *Personality and Individual Differences*, 54, 877–883.

Sulloway, F. J. (1996) *Born to Rebel: Birth Order, Family Dynamics, and Creative Lives*. New York, NY: Pantheon.

Sulloway, F. J. (2020) The evolution of personality. In L. Workman, W. Reader and J. H. Barkow (Eds.), *The Cambridge Handbook of Evolutionary Perspectives on Human Behavior*. Cambridge: Cambridge University Press, pp. 299–310.

Symons, D. (1979) *The Evolution of Human Sexuality*. New York, NY: Oxford University Press.

Szafranski, K., Wetzel, M., Holtze, S., Büntjen, I., Lieckfeldt, D., Ludwig, A., Huse, K., Platzer, M. and Hildebrandt, T. (2022) the mating pattern of captive naked mole-rats is best described by a monogamy model. *Frontiers in Ecology and Evolution*, https://doi.org/10.3389/fevo.2022.855688.

Tajfel, H. (1970) Experiments in intergroup discrimination. *Scientific American*, 223, 96–102.

Tajfel, H., Billig, M. G., Bundy, R. P. and Flament, C. (1971) Social categorization and intergroup behaviour. *European Journal of Social Psychology*, 1(2), 149–178.

Taylor, S. and Workman, L. (2023) *Psychopathy: The Basics*. London: Routledge.

Tennie, C., Call, J. and Tomasello, M. (2009) Ratcheting up the ratchet: on the evolution of cumulative culture. *Philosophical Transactions of the Royal Society B: Biological Sciences*, 364(1528), 2405–2415.

Toates, F. (2014) *How Sexual Desire Works: The Enigmatic Urge*. Cambridge: Cambridge University Press.

Tomasello, M. (1999) *The Cultural Origins of Human Cognition*. Cambridge, MA: Harvard University Press.

Tomasello, M. (2014) The ultra-social animal. *European Journal of Social Psychology*, 44 (3), 187–194.

Trivers, R. L. (1971) The evolution of reciprocal altruism. *Quarterly Review of Biology*, 46, 35–57.

Trivers, R. L. (1972) Parental investment and sexual selection. In B. Campbell (Ed.), *Sexual Selection and the Descent of Man 1871–1971*. Chicago, IL: Aldine Press, pp. 136–179.

Troisi, A. (2020) Are we on the verge of Darwinian psychiatry? In L. Workman, W. Reader and J. H. Barkow (Eds.), *The Cambridge Handbook of Evolutionary Perspectives on Human Behavior*. Cambridge: Cambridge University Press.

Tulving, E. (1972) Episodic and semantic memory. In E. Tulving and W. Donaldson, *Organization of Memory*. New York, NY: Academic Press.

Turkheimer, E. (2000) Three laws of behavior genetics and what they mean. *Current Directions in Psychological Science*, 9(5), 160–164.

Twenge, J. M. (2015) Time period and birth cohort differences in depressive symptoms in the U.S., 1982–2013. *Social Indicators Research*, 121, 437–454.

Van Valen, L. (1973) A new evolutionary law. *Evolutionary Theory*, 1, 1–30.

Velkley, R. L. (2002) *Being after Rousseau: Philosophy and Culture in Question*. Chicago, IL: University of Chicago Press.

Von Frisch, K. (1955) *The Dancing Bees*. New York, NY: Harcourt, Brace.

von Hippel, W. (2018) *The Social Leap: The New Evolutionary Science of Who We Are, Where We Came From, and What Makes Us Happy*. New York, NY: HarperCollins.

Voracek, M., Fisher, M. and Shackelford, T. K. (2009) Sex differences in subjective estimates of non-paternity rates in Austria. *Archives of Sexual Behavior*, 38: 652–656.

Waitt, C., Little, A. C., Wolfensohn, S., Honess P., Brown, A. P., Buchanan-Smith, H. M. and Perrett, D. I. (2003) Evidence from rhesus macaques suggests that male coloration plays a role in female primate mate choice. *Proceedings of the Royal Society of London, Series B: Biological Sciences* 270 (supplement 2): S144–S146.

Walter, K. V., Conroy-Beam, D. Buss, D. M. et al. (2020) Sex differences in mate preferences across 45 countries: a large-scale replication. *Psychological Science*, 31, 408–423.

Wason, P. C. (1966) Reasoning. In B. Foss (Ed.), *New Horizons in Psychology*, Harmondsworth, UK: Penguin.

Waynforth, D. (2001) Mate choice trade-offs and women's preference physically attractive men. *Human Nature*, 12, 207–219.

Weinstein, Y., Bugg, J. M. and Roediger, H. L. (2008) Can the survival recall advantage be explained by basic memory processes? *Memory and Cognition*, 36(5), 913–919.

Whiten, A., Goodall, J., McGrew, W. C., Nishida, T., Reynolds, V., Sugiyama, Y., Caroline, E. G., Wrangham, R. W. and Boesch, C. (1999) Cultures in chimpanzees. *Nature*, 399(6737), 682–685.

WHO. (2008) *The Global Burden of Disease 2004 Update*. Geneva: World Health Organization.

WHO. (2012) *WHO Depression Factsheet October 2012*. Geneva: World Health Organization.

Wilkinson, G. S. (1984) Reciprocal food sharing in the vampire bat. *Nature*, 308(5955), 181–184.

Williams, G. C. (1966) *Adaptation and Natural Selection: A Critique of Some Current Evolutionary Thought*. Princeton, NJ: Princeton University Press.

Williams, G. C. (1975) *Sex and Evolution*. Princeton, NJ: Princeton University Press.

Wilson, E. O. (1975) *Sociobiology: The New Synthesis*. Cambridge, MA: Harvard University Press.

Wilson, E. O. and MacArthur, R. H. (2016) *The Theory of Island Biogeography*. Princeton, NJ: Princeton University Press.

Wolf, M. and McNamara, J. M. (2012) On the evolution of personalities via frequency-dependent selection. *American Naturalist*, 179, 679–692.

Workman, L. (2014) *Charles Darwin: Shaper of Evolutionary Thinking*. London: Palgrave Macmillan.

Workman, L. (2016) Biparental care. In T. Shackelford and V. Weekes-Shackelford (Eds.), *Encycopedia of Evolutionary Psychological Science*. Berlin: Springer.

Workman, L. (2020) Are we still evolving? *Psychology Review*, 25(3), 8–11.

Workman, L. and Reader, W. (2015) *Evolution and Behavior*. London: Routledge.

Workman, L. and Reader, W. (2021) *Evolutionary Psychology* (4th edn.) Cambridge: Cambridge University Press.

Workman, L., Reader, W. and Barkow, J. H. (Eds.) (2020) *Cambridge Handbook of Evolutionary Perspectives on Human Behavior*. Cambridge: Cambridge University Press.

Workman, L. and Taylor, S. (2021) Nature loads the gun, the environment pulls the trigger: The interactive nature of evolutionary psychology. *Open Access Journal of Behavioural Science & Psychology*, 4(3), 180062.

Workman, L. and Taylor, S. (2023) Did Darwin foreshadow evolutionary psychology? *Open Access Journal of Behavioural Science & Psychology*, 6(1), 180074.

Workman, L., Taylor, S. and Barkow, J. H. (2022) Evolutionary perspectives of social development. In P. K. Smith and C. H. Hart (Eds.), *Wiley-Blackwell Handbook of Childhood Social Development*. Hoboken, NJ: Wiley-Blackwell, pp. 84–100.

Wrangham, R. (2009) *Catching Fire: How Cooking Made Us Human*. New York, NY: Basic Books.

Wynn, K. (1995) Origins of numerical knowledge. *Mathematical Cognition*, 1(1), 35–60.

Wynne-Edwards, V. C. (1962) *Animal Dispersion in Relation to Social Behaviour*. Edinburgh: Oliver & Boyd.

Yang, J., Benyamin, B., McEvoy, B. P., Gordon, S., Henders, A. K., Nyholt, D. R., Madden, P. A., Heath, A. C., Martin, N. G., Montgomery, G. W., Goddard, M. E. and Visscher, P. M. (2010) Common SNPs explain a large proportion of the heritability for human height. *Nature Genetics*, 42(7), 565–569.

Zanette, L. Y., Hobbs, E. C., Witterick, L. E., MacDougall-Shackleton, S. A. and Clinchy, M. (2019) Predator-induced fear causes PTSD-like changes in the brains and behaviour of wild animals. *Scientific Reports*, 9(1), 1–10.

Ziker, J., and Schnegg, M. (2005) Food sharing at meals: Kinship, reciprocity, and clustering in the Taimyr Autonomous Okrug, northern Russia. *Human Nature*, 16(2), 178–210.

Zuc, M. and Simmons, L. W. (2018) *Sexual Selection: A Very Brief Introduction*. Oxford: Oxford University Press.

INDEX